HOW TO USE FINANCIAL STATEMENTS

A Guide to Understanding the Numbers

About the Author . . .

James Bandler is president and chief executive officer of Joseph Bandler Corporation, a private investment management company. Previously, he was executive vice president and senior credit officer for City National Bank in Beverly Hills, California. He received his MBA from Harvard University, his BA With Distinction from Stanford University, and is a former member of Robert Morris Associates Professional Bankers' Association. Mr. Bandler's investment opinions and research have been published in *The Wall Street Transcript* and *The Wall Street Journal.*

HOW TO USE FINANCIAL STATEMENTS

A Guide to Understanding the Numbers

James Bandler

McGraw-Hill

*New York   San Francisco   Washington, D.C.   Auckland   Bogotá
Caracas   Lisbon   London   Madrid   Mexico City   Milan
Montreal   New Delhi   San Juan   Singapore
Sydney   Tokyo   Toronto*

McGraw-Hill

A Division of The **McGraw·Hill** Companies

Library of Congress Cataloging-in-Publication Data

Bandler, James.
    How to use financial statements: a guide to understanding the numbers/James Bandler.
        p.   cm.
    Includes index.
    ISBN 0-7863-0197-X
    1. Financial statements.   I. Title.
HF5681.B2B285   1994
657'.3—dc20   94–4756

Printed in the United States of America
        5   6   7   8   9   0   DOC   1   0   9   8

Dedicated to
Scott and Laura

My thanks to Rocky Higgins for making this book possible and for his guidance throughout its composition. Thanks also to Steve Brown for his graphics and illustrations as well as his suggestions. Above all, thanks to my wife, Dianne, for putting up with the eccentricities of one who aspires to write.

Preface

Clearly you are neither a certified public accountant nor a securities analyst. Otherwise you would have picked up a much heavier book with lots of esoteric formulas and equations. More likely you have recently decided that you would like to learn what you really need to know about how to read a financial statement without investing several months of your time and getting so confused and frustrated that you give it up. That's good, because it means that this book can help you.

You're already a step ahead of the pack. Most people who need to understand financial statements don't even realize it. Maybe you just got a job or a promotion into a job in which it would be advantageous to have some familiarity with financial statements. Maybe you have accumulated enough savings to begin looking at investment alternatives, or maybe you have suffered the loss of that member of the family who has always dealt with financial matters.

Needs such as these are common and fairly obvious, but what about those of you who have jobs in completely nonfinancial areas and no interest in investments? The first company whose financial statements you need to understand may well be your own. Will it still be around in five years? Will substantial cuts in its work force be required for it to survive? Will you still have a job? How safe are your medical and retirement benefits?

In recent times, we have seen too many instances of people losing things they had taken for granted: job security, benefits assumed to be guaranteed, even opportunity. And the same questions you would ask about your own company, you need to ask about any other company that you might consider as a prospective employer. Yes, you need to know about financial statements, but you also need instruction that is quick and easy to follow.

For most of us, life is already far more complicated than it needs to be. We are asked to read and understand insurance policies and income tax returns, which were most certainly devised by people whose sole purpose is to confuse us. When is the last time you bought a new issue of a stock or bond and actually read the prospectus? You're lucky if you even get the thing until well after you've made the purchase. If you're thinking of reading the owner's manual for that new computer you just bought, forget it. Find someone who already knows how to work it. Most people, in fact, don't know how to program their VCRs. Too many features and too many things can go wrong. Maybe you can time record the program you want and actually get it right 50 percent of the time. That's pretty good.

In times like these, we need to focus on eliminating unnecessary complication from our lives. Too much of our instructional literature takes things that ought to be easy to understand and makes them more complicated. Or it takes things that are complicated and explains them in complicated ways. In either case, we are more confused than we ought to be.

The purpose of this book is to take a subject that can seem very complicated and make it simple. This sounds like heresy in this day and age, but it is my mission.

James Bandler

Contents

Chapter One

What Are Financial Statements and What Do They Tell Us?

It has been said that an accountant is one who knows the price of everything and the value of nothing. It has also been said that an expert is one who knows more and more about less and less. You should therefore be thankful that it is not my intention to turn you into an expert accountant. It is sufficient that you come to understand the financial statements that the accountants spew forth.

Financial statements are the universally accepted tool for analysis of a business entity. Properly understood, they let us know how good a company looks and how well it has been doing. The financial statements of a business consist of three separate but interrelated reports:

1. The Statement of Financial Position or Balance Sheet.
2. The Profit and Loss or Income Statement.
3. The Statement of Cash Flows.

A complete set of financial statements for The Easy Company, a manufacturer of user-friendly toothpicks, is presented in Exhibit 1–1. Take a moment to look them over because we will refer to them throughout this book.

The purpose of financial statements is to provide the user with a set of data that, in summary form, fairly represents

EXHIBIT 1–1

THE EASY COMPANY
Statement of Financial Position
(December 31)

		1991		1992	Changes
Current Assets:					
Cash		$2,000		$ 900	(1,100)
Marketable securities		1,000		1,000	
Accounts receivable		2,000		2,500	500
Inventory		2,000		2,300	300
Prepaid expenses		100		100	
Total current assets		7,100		6,800	
Investment in Affiliated Co	5,000	200		200	
Property, plant, and equipment					
Cost			6,000		
Accumulated depreciation	3,000	2,000	3,200	2,800	800
Other assets		200		200	
Total assets		9,500		10,000	
Accounts payable		300		500	200
Accrued expenses		1,300		1,200	(100)
Current portion long-term debt		200		200	
Total current liabilities		1,800		1,900	
Long-term debt		2,000		1,800	(200)
Owners' equity:					
Capital stock	2,000		2,000		
Retained earnings	3,700	5,700	4,300	6,300	600
Total Liabilities and owners' equity		$9,500		$10,000	

Statement of Profit and Loss
For the Year Ended December 31, 1992

Net sales	$	$10,000
Cost of goods sold		7,000
Gross profit		3,000
Operating expenses:		
Selling, general, and administrative	1,600	
Depreciation	200	1,800
Profit from operations		1,200

EXHIBIT 1-1 (*concluded*)

Interest expense	200
Income before taxes	1,000
Income tax expense	400
Net profit	$ 600

Statement of Cash Flows

Cash flow from operations:	
Net profit	$ 600
Depreciation	200
	800
Changes to operating assets and liabilities:	
Accounts receivable	(500)
Inventory	(300)
Accounts payable	200
Accrued expenses	(100)
Net cash provided by operations	100
Cash flows from investing activities:	
Additions to property, plant, and equipment	(1,000)
Net cash from financing activities:	
Repayment of long-term debt	(200)
Net cash provided (used)	$(1,100)

the financial strength and performance of a business. Prepared and used properly, they reveal opportunities and provide protection against financial pitfalls. The continuing process of developing and compiling the numbers to be used in the financial presentation is called *accounting*. Frustrated students of accounting have called it many other things, but most of them are unprintable in a snooty book such as this one.

The Balance Sheet provides a snapshot of a company's financial strength as of a given point in time. It lists the company's assets and the portions of these assets financed by liabilities and owners' equity. The dollar amounts of the various accounts in these categories are influenced by how efficiently the company manages them, how it finances its operations, and how profitable it is.

The Income Statement shows how profitable the company was over a specified period of time. It shows the company's revenues, costs of doing business, and net profits.

The Statement of Cash Flows tells us how much cash the company generated over the period covered by the Income Statement and where it went, which is usually quite different from the amount of income (profit). (See Exhibit 1–2.) The various causes of these differences and the ways we measure the dollar impact of each of them will be discussed in Chapters Three through Six. Exhibits 1–2 and 1–3 illustrate the relationship between the three principal reports in the financial statements.

Otherwise sane people often argue about which of the three reports is the most important. Those addicted to the Balance Sheet say that it shows where the company stands after giving effect to everything that has happened in the Income Statement and Cash Flow Statement to date. To them, the Balance Sheet represents the true value of the company.

Fans of the Income Statement sneer at these contentions and regard the Balance Sheet crowd as out of touch. "Hey, you go into business to make money, don't you? The Income Statement tells you how much you're making, so who needs a Balance Sheet? Take that stuff and get out of here."

The cash flow folks see themselves as the truly progressive force in an otherwise Neanderthal system of financial reporting. They believe that "cash is king." Know where cash comes from and where it goes, and you know all that's important about the business.

The cash crowd generally supports liberal causes and tends to be a trifle elitist. "What you want from your busi-

EXHIBIT 1–2
The Interrelationship between the Balance Sheet and Income Statement (The Easy Company)

1992 Sales

December 31, 1992

December 31, 1991

Cash	Accounts Payable
Marketable Securities	Accrued Expenses
	C.P.L.T.D.*
Accounts Receivable	Long-Term Liabilities
Inventory	Owners' Equity
Property, Plant, and Equipment	
Other Assets	

Cost of Goods Sold

Operating Expenses

Interest and Taxes

1992 Net Profit

Cash	Accounts Payable
Marketable Securities	Accrued Expenses
	C.P.L.T.D.*
Accounts Receivable	Long-Term Liabilities
Inventory	Owners' Equity
Property, Plant, and Equipment	
Other Assets	1992 Net Profit

1992 Net Profit becomes part of Owners Equity

*Current Portion of Long-Term Debt.

EXHIBIT 1-3

Relationship between Balance Sheet, Income Statement, and Cash Flow Statement (The Easy Company)

Balance Sheet as of December 31, 1991		Balance Sheet as of December 31, 1992

◄——— Income Statement from January 1, 1992, to December 31, 1992 ———►

FULL YEAR 1992

◄——— Cash Flow Statement from January 1, 1992, to December 31, 1992 ———►

Financial Statement Reports:

• *The Balance Sheet states the financial condition of the Easy Company at a point in time. This point happens to be each New Year's Eve, December 31st.*

• *The last day of the calendar year is the close of Easy Company's accounting period. Other companies may choose different accounting year-ends for various business purposes.*

• *The Income Statement measures the profitability of the Easy Company over a period of time. This period of time begins on January 1st and ends on December 31st of each accounting year.*

• *The Cash Flow Statement explains cash generated and spent by the Easy Company over this same period.*

ness after all is said and done is cash. What good are profits if you can't get any cash out of them? You got a problem with that?''

In fact, each of these financial reports tells a part of a story. Viewed together, they give the reader a complete financial picture of the company. As you increase your understanding of their interrelationship and interdependence, you will become one of the truly enlightened and come to scoff at those radical elements who advocate one report over another.

In addition to the three principal financial reports, most financial statements include a Statement of Changes in Owners' or Shareholders' Equity, which shows increases to the value of ownership through income or ownership interests sold by the company and decreases caused by things like operating losses and dividends paid to shareholders. This report will receive far less emphasis here, as it is fairly straightforward at the level of sophistication we seek to achieve.

Chapter Two

Who Uses Financial Statements and What Do They Look For?

Conventional wisdom has it that only econonerds, masochists, and the terminally boring read financial statements. Not so. Rational and exciting people like you and me not only read them but also find them both interesting and useful.

The principal users of financial statements are probably lenders and investors, but other users of financial statements include owners and managers, customers, suppliers, and even plaintiffs in lawsuits and their attorneys (see Exhibit 2–1). Each of these groups includes potential as well as actual participants. (How do you know whether you want to become a lender or investor until you look at the financial statements? Why sue someone who can't pay?)

All of these groups are probably interested in all of the financial statements, but some tend to place different emphasis on the various components. Even within a given user category, individuals differ with respect to where they place the most emphasis. The following are therefore somewhat generalized characterizations that do not apply in every case.

EXHIBIT 2–1
Who Uses Financial Statements and What Do They Look For?

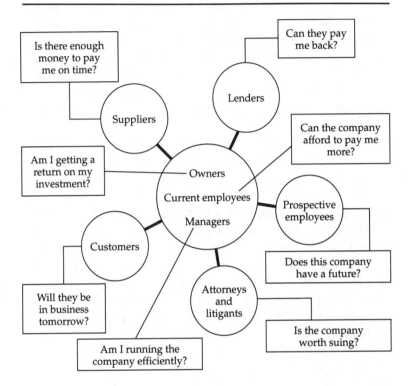

OWNERS

There is a fairly clear distinction between certain interests of lenders to a company and those of owners of a company. (Investors in a company are owners, even though their ownership interests may be very small.) Owners are primarily interested in profitability, as that is what will ultimately add value to their investments. Balance sheet strength and cash flow are usually important only insofar as they are needed to support the continuation of the profit-generating activities.

An exception to this rule is a company being viewed in a liquidation scenario, which is to say that the assets are to be sold, the debts paid, and operations terminated. In this case, the amount by which the value of the assets exceeds the liabilities is the critical factor, since the difference, the equity, is what is available to the owner/investor. The balance sheet therefore takes precedence over the other financial reports.

Another exception might exist in a situation where a company is being considered for acquisition by another company or by large investors. The balance sheet could assume greater importance as a means of determining liquidation value or the value of assets to be acquired.

There are also some kinds of companies for which cash flow may be seen as a better indicator of operating performance than profits due to unusually large noncash charges against profits resulting more from accounting conventions than from performance issues. It is often debatable, however, as to where to draw the line in accepting cash flow instead of profits, as we shall see.

None of this is to suggest that investors disregard or should disregard balance sheets or cash flow. It is just that their primary emphasis tends to be on profits, both actual and expected. They are therefore most interested in the income statement.

LENDERS

How do lenders feel about profits? They like profits too. In most cases losses will make it more difficult for them to be repaid. On the other hand, a company with a very strong balance sheet can withstand small to moderate losses for a period of time without substantially impairing its ability to meet its obligations. Ultimately, however, cash flow is what really repays debt.

Lenders therefore tend to be more interested in the balance sheet and the statement of cash flow than they are in the income statement unless the income statement is so poor that it is obvious that it will soon affect each of the other statements. Profits beyond a certain point become irrelevant to lenders, unlike investors. Lenders don't get paid any more if a company is immensely profitable than they do if it is sufficiently profitable. Investor/owners, on the other hand, gain from every incremental increase in profits—at least theoretically.

MANAGERS

Managers, who are often also owners, need financial statements to assess the performance and strength of their businesses. Is performance as good as they think it is, or are skyrocketing sales only generating increasing losses as costs balloon out of control and inefficiencies abound? If there are problems, how can the financial statements be used to identify them so that they can be corrected? We will explore these subjects in some detail in Chapter Twelve.

SUPPLIERS

Suppliers generally sell to their customers on terms that permit payment at a later date. They therefore need to be concerned with the customer's ability to make these payments when due, just as a lender needs to be concerned about repayment of his debt. Both lenders and suppliers may therefore be called creditors of a company, and their relative interests in the components of the financial statements tend to be similar.

Suppliers, however, may place even less emphasis on profit and loss since their credit tends to be very short term. They can also generally retrieve the goods shipped if payment is not made, and they earn far greater profits from the sale of products than lenders do from financing their purchase. In other words, suppliers have a greater interest in doing the transaction and less risk of loss on it. Suppliers are therefore probably slightly less dependent on financial statements in general than are investors and lenders but are nevertheless among their principal users.

CUSTOMERS

The customers of a company may not at first glance appear to be as likely to be interested in the financial statements of a firm from which they buy, but, if that company is a key supplier of a vital product or service, the customer needs to know that its supplier is of sufficient financial strength to remain in business. A company should not, for example, contract for its data processing services with another company that is not likely to survive for more than a few months. In many instances, customers will therefore at least glance at balance sheets and income statements and in some cases do a more in-depth analysis of the complete financials.

ATTORNEYS AND LITIGANTS

Finally, litigants and their attorneys should have a keen interest in the ability of their target defendant to pay before they commit to the time and expense of litigation. Generally, financial substance will help determine who will be named in a lawsuit. Except in rare cases, financial analysis for this purpose will be fairly superficial and perhaps largely confined to the balance sheet. When in doubt, the lawyers will go after everyone in sight and hope for the best.

EMPLOYEES AND JOB SEEKERS

The importance of understanding the financial condition and performance of an employer or potential employer has become far more critical in recent years than ever before. Whether your company is likely to grow or to shrink in size has important implications for your opportunities for advancement and, indeed, for the security of your job. More to the point, it is becoming increasingly evident that many companies that have thrived in the past will not even be able to continue to be in business in the years to come.

Retirement benefits, such as pensions and postretirement medical benefits, are only as assured as the company's ability to provide for them. The future costs of these benefits, which may or may not be fully funded today, will probably require continued contributions from the company's income and cash. An employee needs to know whether the company at which he works or seeks to work can provide the job and retirement security he deserves for his years of effort.

Clearly there may be other users of financial statements in addition to the ones named above. Government agencies, for example, may be keenly interested in the structure and profitability of a business for purposes of taxation, antitrust implications, or simply negotiating terms of government contracts. The foregoing examples alone, however, suggest a very wide range of usage.

Chapter Three

An Introduction to the Accrual Concept

Before we discuss financial statements in detail, it should be helpful to introduce briefly the concept of accrual accounting and reporting upon which proper financial statements are based. It is essential to the accrual concept to understand the distinctions between *recognizing* revenue for financial reporting and receiving cash and between *incurring* an expense and the payment of cash.

Simply stated, revenue can be recognized when sales are consummated or services provided that create an obligation on the part of the customer to make payment for the sales or services. That is when the revenue is deemed to have been earned.

Similarly, expenses are incurred as assets are used to produce revenue or when the benefit of services received creates an obligation to make payment. Thus, accrual accounting attempts to match expenses with the revenues they generate regardless of when cash is actually paid or received. In practice, there are numerous accounting guidelines that define when these obligations are created and expenses incurred for different types of transactions.

Accountants love accrual accounting. It's fairly complicated and, to them, just a heck of a lot of fun.

Now let's take a look at a financial statement in its simplest and, to most people, its most familiar form.

CASH BASIS FINANCIAL STATEMENTS

John Smith earns $50,000 per year and spends $45,000 of it. (In this example, we will not worry about how he spends it.) He owns a home worth $150,000, against which he owes a $100,000 mortgage to the bank. He has $10,000 in the bank and no other debts. John's financial statement appears below:

Balance Sheet

Assets:
Cash in bank	$ 10,000
Personal residence	150,000
Total assets	$160,000

Liabilities and equity:
Mortgage on personal residence	$100,000
Total liabilities	100,000
Equity	60,000
Total liabilities and equity	$160,000

Income Statement

Total revenue	$50,000
Expenses	45,000
Net income	$ 5,000

Statement of Cash Flow

Cash flow from net income	$5,000

Note that John's cash flow is simply his income. That is because, like most individuals, he reports his income on a cash basis, which means that he only reports as revenue that which is received in cash during the reporting period and as expenses that which is paid in cash.

Suppose John completed a $10,000 consulting job in December but hadn't been paid by year-end. John's cash basis accounts rightfully exclude this income. But if John's goal is to assess what kind of year he had, might it not be reasonable to include the $10,000 earned but not yet received? Indeed it would, and this is where accrual accounting comes in.

Let's also assume that John has a $700 mortgage payment which was due in the last month of the year but which John was unable to pay until a few weeks into the following year. John's accrual basis net income would then become $14,300, consisting of the $5,000 in net cash received plus the $10,000 consulting fee earned but not received less the $700 expense that was not paid when due. His net cash flow, however, would be unaffected since cash for the consulting job was not received and the cash payment for the mortgage was not made during the accounting period. His statement of cash flows might then appear as follows:

Cash flow from net income	$14,300
Cash flow from increase in consulting fee receivable	(10,000)
Cash flow from mortgage expense due but not paid during period	700
Net cash flow	$ 5,000

As demonstrated above, one source of cash is not paying your bills. We will explore this and other aspects of cash flow in Chapter Six.

At first glance, cash accounting makes sense. It seems both logical and simple. Revenue, which may be defined as funds earned from the sale of product or performance of services, is measured by the amount of cash received for these products and services. Similarly, expenses are measured by the amount of cash paid.

Revenue = Cash received
Expense = Cash paid

THE TROUBLE WITH CASH
BASIS ACCOUNTING

The problem with cash accounting is that revenue may be earned and cash payments made for all expenses needed to generate that revenue well before the revenue is received in cash. As in the case of John Smith's consulting fees, not recognizing revenue when it is earned distorts the true operating performance of the company.

Similarly, on a cash basis, expenses could easily be distorted by the timing of cash payments for products purchased or services received. We have seen the obvious example where cash basis income is increased by simply delaying the payment of bills.

ACCRUAL ACCOUNTING TO
THE RESCUE

Accrual accounting focuses on the economic substance of the event instead of just the movement of cash. It recognizes that revenue may be earned before or after cash is received and that revenue should be reported when it is earned, not when cash is received. Accrual accounting also means that expenses are incurred and recorded at the time supplies and materials are shipped or consumed or the benefit of services is received by a company, whether or not cash payment is made at that time.

Under accrual accounting, purchases generally become expenses at the time the materials are used or consumed in the process of generating revenue. This matching of expenses with the revenue they generate is, in fact, a fundamental principle of accrual accounting.

Between the time of purchase and the recording of an expense, the materials acquired are added to inventory. An exception to this matching practice occurs when there is no precise connection between use of the materials and the revenues generated.

For plant and equipment, which generate revenues over a period of years, the cost of their purchase is recognized over their productive (i.e., revenue-generating) life. The cost of plant and equipment is therefore recorded as an asset, the value of which is gradually reduced by expense charges, called *depreciation,* over its useful life.

All of this means that, when Company A ships recreational explosives to Company B, it sends an invoice, which serves to record or recognize the transaction on the books of both companies. Company A records a sale (income statement) and an account receivable (balance sheet), and Company B records a purchase (income statement or balance sheet increase to inventory) and an account payable (balance sheet), even though payment may not be due for 30 days or more. Payments of these amounts will reduce the receivables and increase the cash of Company A while reducing the payables and reducing the cash of Company B. These balance sheet changes have no effect on income and expenses, which are reported at the time of shipment or use of the explosives.

Revenue and expenses are also accrued and reported for amounts that are earned even though no invoice is sent and no accounts receivable or payable are set up. How can this be so? On the income side, a common example might be a company that owns the bonds of the Proprietary Pin Company, which pay interest every six months. Even though the interest is not paid until the end of the six months, it is earned continuously over the six-month period. At the end of three months, the owner or holder of the bonds should show half of the six-month interest payment as income. Since none of this has been received in cash, the amount will be recorded as accrued interest receivable.

One example of an accrued expense would, of course, be this same transaction on the books of the Proprietary

Pin Company, which must record half of the six months of interest as accrued interest expense. Another would be rent that is payable monthly at the end of each month. Halfway through the month, the tenant has received the benefit of occupancy for half the period. He can't move out to avoid paying it. He has therefore incurred an obligation for payment even though he has received no bill or invoice. If he were to prepare financial statements at this time, which is unlikely, he would have to record this amount as an accrued expense both for income and expense reporting as well as for reporting the obligation to pay as a liability on his balance sheet. (If payment is made on or before the end of the month, cash will be reduced and no obligation to pay this amount will appear on the month-end statement.)

ACCRUAL ACCOUNTING AND DEPRECIATION

Accrual accounting requires not only that revenues be recognized in the period in which they are earned but also that expenses be allocated to the periods in which the revenue attributable to them is recognized. Examples of this process, which is called the *matching* of revenues and expenses, can be found in the purchase and use of property, plant, and equipment. These assets may be purchased for cash or some combination of cash and debt in the current reporting period, but they will be used in production, administration, marketing, and distribution for years to come. Since these assets will generate revenues and income in future periods, their costs are matched against the revenues they generate over these periods by means of charges called *depreciation*.

Depreciation is the process by which the cost of an income producing asset is expensed over the useful life of the asset instead of at the time of purchase of the asset. Charging it as an expense at the time of the purchase would result in a tremendous distortion of income, since little of the revenue the asset is expected to produce will be generated in the period of the purchase.

At the end of each period, the amount of depreciation expense is recorded and added to an accumulated depreciation account, the balance of which represents the total of all periodic depreciation charged against assets still owned and in use. This total appears as a reduction to the original purchase price of the asset in arriving at its present book value. The book value is the value on the company's "books," or financial statements, and is based on its historical cost, not its current market value:

Example

Period	Beginning Asset Book Value	Depreciation	Accumulated Depreciation	Ending Asset Book Value
1	10,000	1,000	1,000	9,000
2	9,000	1,000	2,000	8,000
3	8,000	1,000	3,000	7,000
4	7,000	1,000	4,000	6,000
5	6,000	1,000	5,000	5,000

Note that the original beginning asset book value less the accumulated depreciation at the end of any period always equals the ending asset book value for that period.

ACCRUAL ACCOUNTING AND COST OF GOODS SOLD

Another important characteristic of accrual accounting and the matching concept is that the purchase and production costs of inventory are charged as costs of the period in which the inventory is sold, which is not necessarily when it is purchased or produced. All costs of inventory on hand at the beginning of the period as well as inventory produced during the period constitute the cost of inventory available for sale. The cost of inventory on hand at the end of the period is deducted from this total to yield the cost of goods actually sold during the period.

We will discuss these concepts in more detail in Chapters Four through Six. It will suffice for now if you understand that under cash accounting revenues, expenses, assets, and equity are recorded when payments are made in cash, and under accrual accounting they are recorded when they are earned or incurred, regardless of when actual cash payment is made.

If you made it through this chapter with only a mild headache, you're off to a good start.

Chapter Four

The Statement of Financial Position or Balance Sheet

The Statement of Financial Position, more commonly referred to as the Balance Sheet, lists and totals the assets, liabilities, and owners' equity of a company as of the end of an operating period. The owners' equity is the estimated value of the company's assets after deducting all liabilities or, in other words, the accounting estimate of the value of the owners' interest in the company after the creditors are all allotted their share of its assets. The operating period may be one month, three months, a multiple of three months, or one year.

For example, let's assume that we have $50,000 with which to start a business and that we do so by depositing these funds in a bank account as our capital contribution. Our beginning Balance Sheet would appear as follows:

| Cash | 50,000 | Owners' equity | 50,000 |

In this instance, all of the owners' equity consists of contributed capital, which is normally only one component of owners' equity. Once the company has had time to generate profits and losses, these amounts will be reflected through the retained earnings section of owners' equity.

Next we decide to lease a store site, but we need to purchase $40,000 in furnishings, fixtures, and equipment to operate the store. Since we also know that we will need about $20,000 in beginning inventory and some cash to meet operating needs, we choose to borrow $20,000 of the $40,000 and pay the balance in cash. Our Balance Sheet is now:

Cash	$30,000	Bank loan	$20,000
Property and equipment	40,000	Owners' equity	50,000
	$70,000		$70,000

Now we buy the inventory for $20,000 in cash:

Cash	$10,000		
Inventory	20,000	Bank loan	$20,000
Property and equipment	40,000	Owners' equity	50,000
	$70,000		$70,000

In this simplified illustration, we have ignored the classification of assets and liabilities into current and noncurrent as well as how owners' equity is increased and decreased through profits and losses, all of which is coming up shortly. We have just shown how the business has been started with about 28.6 percent of our assets financed by means of debt and 71.4 percent by our own capital contribution, all the while keeping the Balance Sheet in balance.

WHY WE HAVE BALANCE SHEETS AND WHY THEY BALANCE

Most users of financial statements want to know things like what a business is worth and whether its financial condition is strong enough to withstand adversity and support its growth. That is what the Balance Sheet is supposed to do best, although, as we shall see in subsequent chapters, how well it actually performs this function is subject to the accuracy of certain estimates that are a necessary evil in financial reporting.

Since assets are really what we need to run a business, why do we need liabilities and owners' equity? The problem is that we have to get the assets somehow. They must either be purchased with funds on hand (another asset), exchanged for other assets, or purchased with the proceeds of debt, a liability. The only way to get cash or other assets with which to acquire the asset we need is to have the cash contributed in the form of capital, generated through the profits of the company or, once again, borrowed in the form of liabilities. Since contributed capital and retained earnings are both a part of owners' equity, we need to have liabilities and owners' equity in a combined amount equal to the cost of any assets we own.

The relationship between the three broad categories of the Balance Sheet may be summarized as follows:

Assets − Liabilities = Owners' equity (or net worth)

Similarly, by reshuffling our equation, we can see that:

Assets = Liabilities + Owners' equity

It is for this reason that the Statement of Financial Position is usually referred to as the Balance Sheet. Since the totals of both sections of the statement are always equal, they can be said to be balanced (see Exhibit 4–1).[1]

---

[1] To determine why this statement was never called a Balanc*ed* Sheet would require considerable research and is beyond the scope of this book. However, my own suspicion is that it was the result of a typographical error.

EXHIBIT 4–1
Balancing the Books

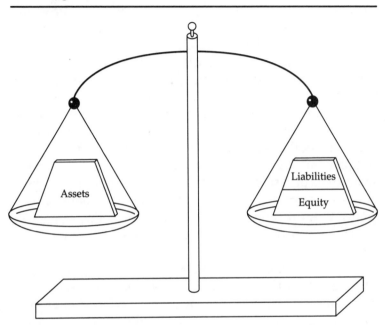

Why are total assets always equal to total liabilities plus net worth? By definition. If you take away what I owe from what I own, what is left is what I am worth (in strictly financial terms).

CURRENT ASSETS

Assets consist of cash, things that can easily be converted to cash, and things that may not be easily converted to cash but are needed to enable the company to make products or provide services for which it will eventually receive cash.

Assets are generally listed in an order that approximates how easily each item can be converted to cash, beginning with cash itself. Assets that can immediately be converted to cash or are expected to be converted to cash within one year are subtotaled and classified as *current* assets. These may include marketable securities, accounts receivable, inventory, and certain prepaid expenses such as insurance or taxes.

If all of these assets are converted into cash within one year, you would expect the company to have a lot of cash at the end of the year. Right? That's not what happens. The company just turns around and puts this cash back into the same kinds of assets so that its business can continue making things or providing services. The cash flow snobs will be happy to show you how you end up with the amount of cash that you do, and we'll take a look at that in Chapter Six.

The Easy Company had $2,000,000 in cash at the end of 1991 and $900,000 at the end of 1992. We shall see in our discussion of cash flow how it used $1,100,000 in cash in spite of profitable operations. (In Exhibit 1–1, we can see under the column headed "Changes" what increases in assets and decreases in liabilities and owners' equity contributed to this net use of cash.)

Marketable securities are usually very short-term obligations of the U.S. government or large corporations. They must be actively traded in markets that provide public price quotations on a continuous basis. Otherwise they're not marketable enough to be called marketable securities.

Accounts receivable are amounts due from customers for products sold or services provided. Revenue from these sales has been *recognized* and income *earned* in the Income Statement, but cash has not yet been received. Remember that revenues and expenses are recognized or accrued at the time a sale or a service provided creates an obligation for payment at a future date.

In fact, some customers never pay, either because their own business is not so hot or because they don't like what you sold them (buyer's remorse). For this reason, there is an allowance for doubtful accounts netted out of the accounts receivable total.

The Easy Company had accounts receivable of $2,000,000 at the end of 1991 and $2,500,000 at the end of 1992. Since sales were $10,000,000 during 1992, that amount was added to receivables during the year (assuming all sales were credit, as opposed to cash, sales). If all receivables had been collected, both the $2,000,000 beginning balance and the $10,000,000 in new sales would be gone from the Balance Sheet by the end of 1992. Since $2,500,000 remains on the books, however, the company must have collected only $7,500,000 of the $10,000,000 in new sales in addition to all of the receivables outstanding at the end of 1991.

A simple formula illustrates the relationship between accounts receivable (AR) outstanding, collection of receivables, and sales:

Beginning AR + Sales − Collections = Ending AR[2]

Any time sales exceed collections, accounts receivable increase. Cash received is then less than sales. In financial jargon, that is a use of cash and represents a reduction of cash flow. Any time collections exceed sales, accounts receivable decrease. Cash received is then greater than sales. That is a source of cash and represents an increase in cash flow.

Inventory consists of products held for sale (finished goods), materials used in production (raw materials), and

---

[2] Write-offs of bad debts, which would also reduce ending accounts receivable, are omitted from this illustration for the sake of simplicity. Otherwise they would be subtracted along with collections.

the value of partially completed products as determined by the amount of labor, materials, and other costs applied to them at their various stages of completion (work-in-process). The Easy Company had $2,000,000 in inventory at the end of 1991 and $2,300,000 at the end of 1992 (see Exhibit 4–2).

As in the case of accounts receivable, there is a basic formula that shows the effects of the production and sale of goods on inventory and the financial statements. Inventory may consist of only purchases, as in the case of a wholesaler or distributor, or of purchases plus manufacturing costs, as in the case of a manufacturer who purchases raw materials that go into the production process. For purposes of our formula, we will call this component *production* instead of just purchases, with the understanding that in some companies it may consist only of purchases. We will also use the notation CGS for the cost of goods sold, which means that portion of beginning inventory plus production during the period that was actually sold during the period. Therefore:

Beginning inventory + Production − CGS = Ending inventory

and therefore:

CGS = Beginning inventory + Production − Ending inventory

The first equation tells us that, if production exceeds the cost of goods sold, ending inventory will be higher than beginning inventory. That means that, on balance, cash went into inventory that was not sold, a use of cash or reduction of cash flow. If, on the other hand, cost of goods sold exceeds

EXHIBIT 4–2
The Three Stages of Inventory (The Easy Company)

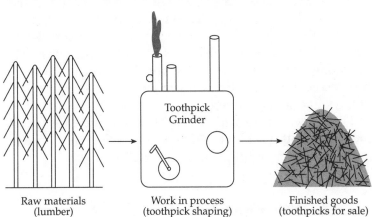

Raw materials   Work in process   Finished goods
(lumber)   (toothpick shaping)   (toothpicks for sale)

production, ending inventory will be less than beginning inventory. Inventory would then be a source of cash and a boost to cash flow.

The second equation is used for the calculation of cost of goods sold for the Income Statement. For The Easy Company, it would appear as follows:

Beginning inventory	$2,000,000
Purchases or production costs	+7,300,000
Cost of goods available for sale	9,300,000
Less: Ending inventory	−2,300,000
Cost of goods sold	$7,000,000

Prepaid expenses may be payments for things like insurance, where the premium is paid in advance for coverage over a future period of time. The premium is earned by the insurance provider evenly over the period of coverage.

Therefore, no expense is recognized by the insured at the time of prepayment.

As the expense is recognized over the period of coverage, however, the amount of the asset, prepaid insurance expense, will decrease while no further cash payments will be made. The prepaid expense will provide cash during the operating period only in the sense that expenses will be recorded in the Income Statement that will not require cash outlays during this period.

The Easy Company had $100,000 in prepaid expenses at the end of both 1991 and 1992, suggesting that prepayments in the same amount were made in each year.

NONCURRENT ASSETS

Noncurrent assets typically include property and equipment used in production, sales, or distribution of products or services. They may also include investments in other companies, most commonly companies affiliated through partial ownership by the reporting company. These assets may provide the means to produce cash during the operating period but are not themselves expected to be converted to cash in this time frame, if at all.

The Easy Company had $2,000,000 in property, plant, and equipment at the end of 1991 and $2,800,000 at the end of 1992. The company purchased $1,000,000 of new property and equipment during 1992, but gross property and equipment was reduced by $200,000 in depreciation. The net figure therefore increased by $800,000, calling for the use of an equal amount of cash:

Beginning property, plant, and equipment	$2,000,000
Add new acquisitions	1,000,000
Less depreciation	(200,000)
Ending property, plant, and equipment	$2,800,000

CURRENT LIABILITIES

Liabilities are amounts that are owed by the company in the form of debt, unpaid bills, and expenses that have been incurred but are not yet payable and/or have not yet been paid. These accrued expenses might typically include amounts payable for wages and salaries earned by employees, interest expense on debt, and rent and utilities expenses. As with assets, amounts payable within one year are classified as current liabilities.

A formula that is similar to our accounts receivable formula describes the effects of changes in accounts payable and other accrued liabilities:

Beginning   balance + Additions – Payments = Ending balance

If additions, or new accruals, exceed payments, cash paid out is less than expenses accrued. As we shall see, that is a source of cash and an increase to cash flow when it comes time to adjust reported income to actual cash flow. Similarly, if payments exceed new accruals, that is a use of cash and represents a reduction of cash flow.

In most companies, current assets must exceed current liabilities by some margin dictated by the operating characteristics of the particular type of business in order for the company to be considered sufficiently liquid. *Liquidity* is a measure of how well a company is able to pay for its short-term cash operating requirements. The more predictable the cash flow generated from the operations of a company, the less the amount of liquidity generally seen to be required in the Balance Sheet.

The amount by which current assets exceed current liabilities is called *working capital*. Any deficiency in current assets compared to current liabilities is called negative or deficit working capital.

The current liabilities of The Easy Company increased from $1,800,000 in 1991 to $1,900,000 in 1992, while its current assets declined from $7,000,000 to $6,800,000 in the same period. It was therefore slightly less liquid at the end of 1992, but its liquidity was still more than adequate with a ratio of current assets to current liabilities of over 3.5 to 1.0.

LONG-TERM DEBT

Long-term debt and other long-term liabilities are obligations that are not scheduled or expected to be paid during the following year. These generally consist of the noncurrent portion of debt owed to banks or other financial institutions and publicly traded bonds or notes representing obligations of the company.

OWNERS' EQUITY

Owners' equity, which is called *shareholders' equity* in the case of a corporation, consists of both funds contributed to the company for the purchase of ownership interests and the accumulation of the profits of the business that have not been paid out to the owners in the form of dividends or other capital distributions. These accounts are called *contributed capital,* or *capital,* and *retained earnings* respectively.

Owners' equity is not itself an asset. It represents the owners' claim on assets after all liabilities are recognized.

LEVERAGE

To the extent that total liabilities are large in relation to owners' equity, a company is said to be *leveraged*. Other things being equal, a company with little leverage is less risky than a company that is highly leveraged. The highly leveraged company has less room to absorb operating losses or other reductions in its asset values and owners' equity than the company with little leverage.

Leverage became a controversial subject during the 1980s, when many companies were acquired by means of leveraged buy outs, or LBOs. The acquirer would borrow against the assets and/or cash flow of the company to obtain the funds with which to purchase its stock. In many cases, this left the acquired company so heavily in debt (i.e., highly leveraged) that it lacked the financial capacity to survive under conditions more adverse than originally projected when the deals were put together.

The Easy Company reduced its total liabilities in 1992 from $3,800,000 to $3,700,000 while increasing its owners' equity from $5,700,000 to $6,300,000 through the retention of $600,000 in 1992 profits. It thus became slightly less leveraged at the end of 1992, though its leverage was quite modest in 1991 as well.

We examine the many ways in which a Balance Sheet may be used to assess the financial health of a company in subsequent chapters.

Chapter Five

The Profit and Loss or Income Statement

The Profit and Loss Statement is intended to show how much money a company is making or losing. It does so by subtracting all of the costs of production of goods that have been sold during the period and other expenses of running the company from the revenues generated from sales of products or from services provided.

The Profit and Loss Statement is sometimes called the Income Statement. The former became the preferred terminology when it became evident that companies could lose money as well as make it. However, the latter is probably more commonly used because it is easier to say.

In Exhibit 1–1, we can see that The Easy Company had sales of $10,000,000 and a net profit of $600,000 after a cost of goods sold of $7,000,000, other operating expenses of $1,800,000, interest expense of $200,000 and a provision for income taxes of $400,000:

Net sales		$10,000,000
Cost of goods sold		7,000,000
Gross profit		$ 3,000,000
Operating expenses:		
Selling, general, and administrative	1,600,000	
Depreciation	200,000	1,800,000
Profit from operations		1,200,000
Interest expense		200,000
Income before taxes		1,000,000

Provision for income taxes   <u>400,000</u>
Net profit   600,000

REVENUES

Since The Easy Company is a manufacturing company, its revenues take the form of products sold, or sales. Revenues, however, are not necessarily synonymous with sales. Revenues can come from rentals, interest earned, commissions, or any one of a number of services for which revenues are not commonly referred to as sales.

The Easy Company sold $10,000,000 in toothpicks during 1992. These sales were net of a small number of toothpicks that were returned by dissatisfied customers, most of whom claimed they were not as "user-friendly" as advertised. Its sales are therefore stated as *net sales*.

COST OF GOODS SOLD

The cost of goods sold is made up of all costs allocated to inventory sold during the period, including labor, materials, and overhead.[1] For The Easy Company, these costs consisted principally of lumber, depreciation of toothpick manufacturing plant and equipment, and wages and salaries of production workers and supervisors.

---

[1] Overhead consists of periodic expenses that are incurred whether or not any sales are made or product produced. Depreciation of property and equipment, rent, and insurance are common examples of overhead.

GROSS PROFITS

The difference between a company's sales and its cost of goods sold is its *gross profit*. It is called gross profit because other expenses still need to be deducted in order to arrive at net profit.

Gross profit represents the contribution revenues make toward coverage of expenses not tied to production and toward net profit. The Easy Company had gross profit of $3,000,000 in 1992 with which to cover other expenses of $2,400,000, leaving a net profit of $600,000.

OPERATING EXPENSES

Operating expenses consist of *general* and *administrative* expenses and *selling* expenses. General and administrative expenses are expenses that are necessary just to keep the business running from day to day even if no sales are made and no products produced. These include management salaries, property and equipment rentals or depreciation, interest expense, utilities not connected with production, most research and development expenses, insurance, office supplies, salaries of office workers, and numerous other items that you really don't need to hear about.

Selling expenses consist of all forms of advertising, the salaries and commissions of sales personnel, and all costs of supporting the sales function. These costs include many of the same items as general and administrative expenses, but only, for example, those portions of office supplies and utilities that were allocated to the sales function.

To aid in the financial analysis of its performance, The Easy Company chose to show $200,000 in depreciation and $200,000 in interest expense separately from selling, general, and administrative expenses. They might just as well have been included in the latter, since they were operating expenses. Had they been costs of production, they would have been included in cost of goods sold.

PROVISION FOR INCOME TAXES

The provision for income taxes, or income tax expense, is based on the company's effective income tax rate applied to its net taxable income. The effective tax rate may be different from the statutory rate. Differences can be caused by various tax credits and items that may be allowable expenses for financial reporting but not for income taxes or allowable for income taxes but not treated as expenses for financial reporting.

The Easy Company's taxes were 40 percent of its income before taxes after allowing for these adjustments.

NET INCOME

Net income is what is left over after all the costs of doing business are deducted from all the revenues earned (see Exhibit 5–1). That portion of net income that is not paid out in dividends or for other unusual things not directly related to running the business becomes a part of owners' equity by way of the retained earnings account.

The Easy Company earned a hefty $600,000 in net profit from selling toothpicks in 1992. It retained every penny of it.

THE INCOME STATEMENT'S IMPACT ON THE BALANCE SHEET

Whenever you earn income or suffer losses, it directly affects your net worth (owners' equity). For this reason,

EXHIBIT 5–1
Sales Breakdown by Expenses and Profit (The Easy Company)

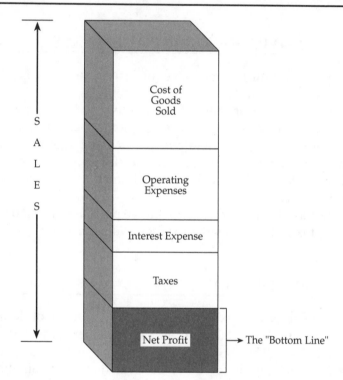

profits and losses are added to or subtracted from owners'
equity and thus affect the Balance Sheet. Increases in owners' equity caused by operating profits may result in increases in cash and/or other assets, decreases in debt, or
some combination of the two. Losses would, of course,
have the opposite effects. Thus the Balance Sheet is kept in
balance. Exhibit 5–2 shows the relationship between major
Income Statement categories and corresponding Balance
Sheet accounts.

EXHIBIT 5-2
The Effect of Income Statement Items on the Balance Sheet

Income Statement		Balance Sheet
Sales	—leads to→	Increase accounts receivable
− Cost of goods sold	—leads to→	Decrease inventory
= Gross profit		
− Operating expenses	—leads to→	Increase accrued expenses
	or	Increase accounts payable
	or	Decrease cash
	or	Decrease prepaid expenses
= Net profit	—leads to→	Increase retained earnings (owners' equity)

Exhibit 5–3 shows in more detail how Income Statement results might affect a company's Balance Sheet. In this example, the Simple Company, a manufacturer of high grade sludge, had sales of $1,000,000 and a net profit of $100,000 after deducting cost of sales (inventory sold) of $600,000 and operating expenses of $300,000.

The company produced $700,000 in inventory during the period, causing an increase in ending inventory of $100,000 after the sale of $600,000 in inventory. It also collected only $800,000 of its receivables. The $200,000 difference between sales and collections during the period caused ending accounts receivable to increase by this amount.

Liabilities had to increase by $200,000 to fund the difference between the $100,000 increase in owners' equity and the $300,000 increase in total assets. This amount also represents a negative cash flow in spite of positive net profits, a scenario we shall explore more in the next chapter.

EXHIBIT 5-3
The Simple Company—$000

Beginning Balance Sheet

Ending Balance Sheet

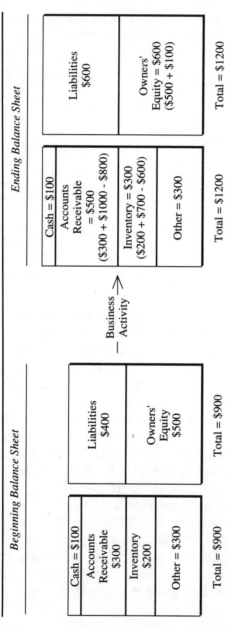

Cash = $100	
Accounts Receivable $300	Liabilities $400
Inventory $200	Owners' Equity $500
Other = $300	
Total = $900	Total = $900

— Business → Activity

Cash = $100	
Accounts Receivable = $500 ($300 + $1000 - $800)	Liabilities $600
Inventory = $300 ($200 + $700 - $600)	Owners' Equity = $600 ($500 + $100)
Other = $300	
Total = $1200	Total = $1200

Business activity assumptions:

1. Sales = $1,000
2. Cost of sales = $600
3. Operating expenses = $300
4. Net profit = $100
5. Inventory produced = $700
6. Account receivable collections = $800

STATEMENT OF CHANGES IN SHAREHOLDERS' EQUITY

A Statement of Changes in Shareholders' Equity for 1992 for The Easy Company, were it to provide one, might appear as follows:

Balance, January 1	$5,700
Add net income	600
Less dividends declared	0
Balance, December 31	$6,300

This information becomes only slightly more exciting when there are sales and/or repurchases of stock or other special charges or allocations between retained earnings and contributed capital. We do not need this extra excitement at our level of discussion, and, for companies like The Easy Company, a Statement of Changes in Shareholders' Equity doesn't really provide any additional information.

Chapter Six

The Statement of Cash Flows

The fact that all revenue is not received when it is earned and all expenses are not paid precisely as incurred is one of the factors giving rise to the need for a statement of cash flows to reconcile the accrual income statement to net cash collected or paid.

The statement of cash flows became a required part of the financial statements fairly recently. Simply put, it shows how the profits or losses during the accounting period combine with all of the balance sheet changes to produce a change in the company's cash balance.

In arriving at the change in cash, changes caused by the day-to-day operations of the business are separated from changes caused by things like investment and financing activities to reveal "cash flow from operations." This subtotal in the overall derivation of cash flow has special significance for many users of financial statements for it essentially converts profits or losses into cash flow. This distinction is important to financial statement users who believe that actual money in the bank is more important as a measure of business performance than some accounting contrivance called profit.

Ironically, the whole accrual accounting system was developed in order to convert cash flow into profits, which were at that time seen as a better measure of performance than net cash received.

CONCEPTUAL BASIS FOR
DETERMINING CASH FLOW

In the case of The Easy Company, it can be seen that profits for the year amounted to $600,000. Were it not for the various accruals necessary to convert profits to cash flow, cash would have increased by the same amount. In fact, cash *decreased* by $1,100,000. How is this possible?

Cash flow from operations:	
Net profit	$ 600
Depreciation	200
	800
Changes to operating assets and liabilities:	
Accounts receivable	(500)
Inventory	(300)
Accounts payable	200
Accrued expenses	(100)
Net cash provided by operations	100
Cash flows from investing activities:	
Additions to property, plant, and equipment	(1,000)
Net cash from financing activities:	
Repayment of long-term debt	(200)
Net cash provided (used)	$(1,100)

Our Cash Flow Statement begins with net income as if all income were received in cash and all expenses paid in cash during the period. It then makes numerous adjustments to reflect the fact that this is not so.

Anytime you have income that does not result in cash received, it is considered a use of cash in the conversion of net profit from the Income Statement to cash provided in the Cash Flow Statement. To illustrate this point, assume that you earned $100 during the accounting period but did not collect it. Your income was $100, but all of it went into increasing your accounts receivable by $100. Your cash flow was zero. The $100 increase in accounts receivable was therefore a use of cash that offset the $100 source from net income.

Similarly, anytime cash is received in a period other than the one in which income was earned, you have a source of cash in the period it is received. If, in the above example, you do nothing in the following accounting period but collect the $100, you will have a source of cash equal to the $100 reduction in accounts receivable but no net income in this period.

Anytime you have an expense that does not result in a cash outlay, it is considered a source of cash in the conversion of net profit from the income statement to cash provided in the Cash Flow Statement. Assume, for example, that you purchase and use $50 of office supplies in an accounting period but have not yet paid for them by the end of the period. Your expense during the period was $50, but all of it went into an increase in your accounts payable. You reconcile the $50 Income Statement expense to actual cash flow by treating the increase in accounts payable as a source of cash. Otherwise the $50, having been deducted in arriving at net income, would stand as a net use of cash by default.

Anytime payment is made in a period other than the one in which the expense is recorded, you have a use of cash in the period payment is made. Again, assume that the $50 for the supplies is paid in the following period. Since cash is paid in this period but no expense is incurred, net income would have to be adjusted by showing the $50 reduction in accounts payable as a use of cash in the Statement of Cash Flows.

All of these timing differences between income earned and cash received, and between expenses incurred and cash paid, result in changes in accruals on the Balance Sheet. Changes in accruals therefore require corresponding adjustments to reported income to arrive at cash flow.

CALCULATING CASH FLOW

To arrive at net profit in the Income Statement, $200,000 in depreciation was deducted as an expense. Remember, however, that depreciation does not represent a cash outlay in this period. It is the amount by which long-lived income-generating assets are reduced in value to reflect a reduction in their useful lives over time. Depreciation is therefore added back into net income as the first step in determining cash flow.

We can also see that accounts receivable increased by $500,000 during the period. This increase represents an increase in the amount of revenues that were not received in cash. Since the Income Statement records all revenues regardless of whether cash has been received, the $500,000 needs to be deducted in our derivation of cash flow.

Inventory increased by $300,000 during the period, and that too represents a use of cash. In our calculation of cost of goods sold on pages 28 and 29, beginning inventory was added to the cost and ending inventory deducted. That is because it is assumed that beginning inventory is in fact sold during the accounting period and therefore is appropriately charged as a cost of sales during the period.

Ending inventory, on the other hand, is, by definition, still there. It therefore cannot be charged against the sales of this period and needs to be deducted from these costs in arriving at cost of goods sold. As a deduction from costs, it represents an increase in income. From a cash perspective, however, it is money out the door.

Beginning inventory, however, represented a cash outlay in a prior period but a cost of sales in the current period. It therefore needs to be added to the cash flow of the current period, so that the adjustment to profits for cash flow from inventory changes is the beginning inventory less the ending inventory. An increase in inventory then represents a decrease in cash flow.

Increases in prepaid items are also uses of cash, since they are cash outlays of the current period for expenses of the following period. Purchases of property and equipment represent uses of cash because they are cash outlays that are depreciated over their lives rather than charged to current expense.

Since depreciation expense has already been added to net income in determining cash flow, accumulated depreciation changes should not be considered as part of cash flow from operations. That would result in double counting of depreciation as a source of cash. Only changes in gross property and equipment are reflected in the cash flow statement. These are shown under cash flows from investing activities.

As we look at these changes in asset accounts, remember that sources of cash are decreases in noncash assets and increases in liabilities or owners' equity, including those that result from net profits. Uses are increases in assets and decreases in liabilities or owners' equity, including those that result from net losses.

These simple truths are the key to understanding cash flow. All loans, for example, are repaid from decreases in assets, increases in other liabilities or increases in owners' equity. Any banker who does not realize this does not really understand his sources of repayment.

The relationship between cash and other balance sheet accounts is illustrated below:

Cash	*Liabilities*
	+ Source of cash
Noncash Assets	− Use of cash
+ Use of cash	
− Source of cash	*Owners' Equity*
	+ Source of cash
	− Use of cash

If any account change shown as a source of cash above takes place and no other account has changed, cash would have to increase in order for the balance sheet to stay in balance. If any account change shown as a use of cash took place and no other account changed, cash would have to decrease to maintain balance.

Exhibit 6–1 shows how all of this works. Six possibilities for changing cash are illustrated graphically, starting with a beginning balance sheet for reference. All increases or decreases in cash result from the indicated changes in these categories.

The first scenario shows a decrease in cash caused by an increase in assets other than cash (a use of cash). This reflects the use of cash to purchase assets or fund increases in assets such as accounts receivable.

The second shows an increase in cash caused by a decrease in noncash assets (source). This would result from the sale of assets such as property and equipment or the conversion, or net reduction, of assets such as inventory and accounts receivable into cash.

The third scenario is a reduction in cash caused by a reduction in owners' equity (use). Most commonly this would be caused by a net operating loss that drew down cash balances in the absence of any other sources of cash. It could also be caused by cash purchases of the company's stock.

The fourth scenario shows an increase in cash caused by an increase in owners' equity (source). This increase could be caused by operating profits or the sale of company stock.

The fifth scenario shows an increase in cash resulting from an increase in liabilities (source). This occurs when a company borrows and holds the proceeds in cash, at least temporarily, or when it funds operating cash needs through increases in accounts payable and other accrued liabilities.

The sixth scenario shows a decrease in cash caused by a decrease in liabilities (use). That would occur when a

EXHIBIT 6–1
How Changes in the Balance Sheet Affect Cash

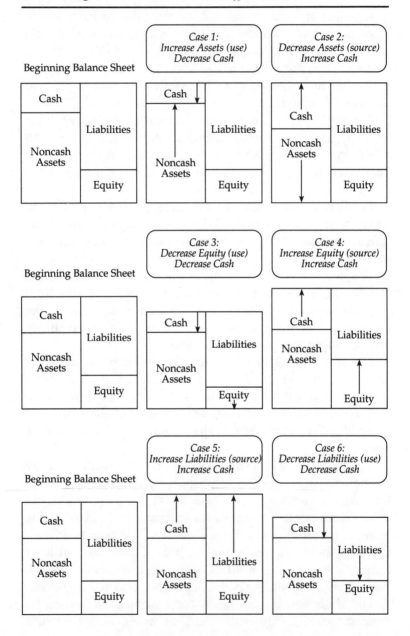

company uses cash to pay down debt, accounts payable, or other accrued liabilities.

Each of the foregoing possibilities shows a source or use of cash resulting in an increase or decrease to the cash balance. If these sources and uses were to partially or wholly offset one another, however, as is usually the case, there might be little or no net change to cash balances.

To demonstrate how offsetting sources or uses might not affect cash, the six scenarios in Exhibit 6–2 show all of the offsetting combinations of changes that will result in no change in cash.

The first is an increase in noncash assets (use) offset by an increase in liabilities (source). In this case, the increase in assets is funded by debt or other liabilities instead of cash.

The second is an increase in assets (use) offset by an increase in equity (source). In this case the asset expansion is funded by profits or a sale of the company's stock.

The third case shows a decrease in assets (source) offset by a decrease in liabilities (use). Here cash that would have resulted from the sale or conversion of assets was instead used to pay liabilities.

The fourth case shows a reduction in assets (source) offset by a reduction in equity (use). That would most commonly represent operating losses funded by the liquidation of assets or conversion (reduction) of inventory and receivables to cash.

The fifth scenario shows an increase in liabilities (source) offset by a decrease in equity (use). Here operating losses or repurchase of the company's stock were most likely funded by the use of debt and other liabilities rather than by cash.

The sixth scenario shows a reduction in liabilities (use) offset by an increase in equity (source). Here cash provided by operating profits and/or sale of stock was used to reduce liabilities.

EXHIBIT 6–2
How Changes in the Balance Sheet Affect Noncash Items

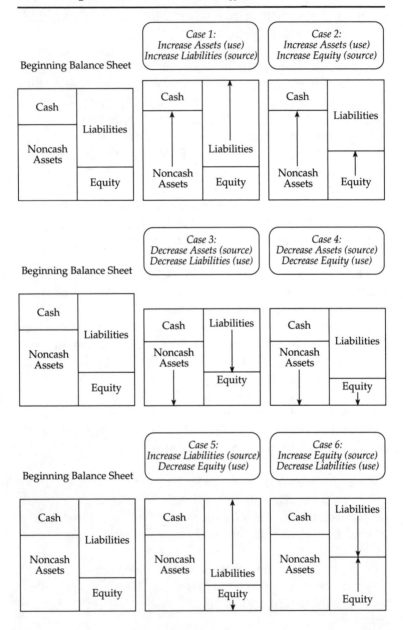

In reality, the changes that take place in cash balances are the result of a myriad of transactions that affect assets, liabilities, and owners' equity during a period. By isolating them into their individual components, however, we can see more clearly how any balance sheet change, including changes in owners' equity caused by profits and losses, will affect cash and cash flow. We can also see how a use that is offset by a noncash source or a source that is offset by a noncash use will have no effect at all.

Hopefully these simple diagrams will serve as a reference to assist you in seeing the impact of any change in a Balance Sheet account or net income or losses on cash flow and cash balances.

Cash flow can therefore be derived purely from computing changes in the Balance Sheet between one period and another for all items except cash. The difference between all sources of cash and all uses is net cash provided or used. The $1.1 million in cash used by The Easy Company, for example, is the residual after netting all other balance sheet changes against one another (see Exhibit 1–1).

However, no adjustment is made in the Cash Flow Statement for the change in retained earnings since it has already been taken into account by starting with the net profit or loss in the derivation of cash flow. It is more instructive for analytical purposes to begin with net income (instead of the increase in owners' equity) and depreciation (instead of the increase in the allowance for depreciation) and then list all other sources and uses of operating cash flow. One can then include investment and financing sources and uses of funds that are not directly related to operating performance during the period and should therefore be analyzed as separate components of cash flow.

Let's look at liabilities and other changes in owners' equity. Increases in accrued liabilities provide cash because they represent expenses charged to income that have not been paid in cash. (Remember, not paying your bills is a source of cash, albeit in a very short-term sense.) Decreases mean that cash has been paid in excess of expenses charged against income, a use of cash vis-à-vis reported profit. Increases in long-term debt provide cash proceeds quite apart from anything that happens in the income statement. These amounts therefore need to be added to income to determine cash as part of net cash from financing activities. Similarly, decreases in long-term debt represent cash used to pay down debt but have no immediate effect on profit or loss. The latter are therefore deducted from cash flow under net cash from financing activities.

The Statement of Cash Flow on page 43 shows how operating performance as well as investments in plant and equipment, and changes in long-term debt affect the Statement of Cash Flow of The Easy Company.

Although not present in the financial statements of The Easy Company, dividends and capital distributions would reduce owners' equity and cash as they represent cash paid out after the determination of net income. Capital contributed through the sale of ownership interests, such as public stock offerings, would increase cash from sources independent of income statement (operating) activities.

ALTERNATIVE FORMAT FOR STATEMENT OF CASH FLOWS

There is another method of presentation for the Statement of Cash Flows. In the opinion of this author, which carries a lot of weight here, it is not nearly as good as the one we have just seen. This second method is intended to show how much cash was generated from sales, how much was used in production, and how much was used in other operating expenses. At each step, revenues earned or expenses incurred are converted into cash received or cash paid.

To adjust our accrual statement revenues to cash collected during the period, we must add in accounts receivable at the beginning of the period even though they were earned in a prior period. They are presumed to be the first monies collected. We then add revenues earned during the period as if they had all been collected. We then subtract accounts receivable at the end of the period as these represent the amount of the first two items which clearly was not collected:

$$\text{Cash revenue} = \text{Accrual revenue} + \text{Beginning AR} - \text{Ending AR}$$

Similarly, costs of goods sold are converted to actual cash outlays for production. Cash paid for materials consists of beginning accounts payable plus purchases less ending accounts payable. Labor and overhead costs are similarly adjusted to show only those amounts paid in cash.

Operating expenses are also adjusted by adding the total of beginning accrued expenses and deducting the total of ending accrued expenses. The resulting Statement of Cash Flows for The Easy Company would then look something like this:

Cash received from revenues	$ 9,500
Cash paid for production costs	(7,100)
Cash paid for operating expenses	(2,300)
Cash derived from operations	100
Cash paid for property, plant, and equipment	(1,000)
Cash paid for debt reduction	(200)
Net cash flow	$(1,100)

---

[1] Cost of goods sold + Increase in inventory − Increase in accounts payable.

[2] SG&A expenses + Interest expense + Inome taxes paid + Decrease in accrued expenses.

My principal objection to this format is that I'm not sure it tells me anything I really need to know. Our earlier format started with net income plus noncash accounting charges that had reduced net income but not required cash outlays. (The total of these two numbers would represent cash flow in the absence of any other balance sheet changes.) It then showed how Balance Sheet changes, reflecting changes in cash receipt and payment patterns, altered this amount to arrive at actual cash flow from operations. Finally, it showed cash used for investments and debt payments and thereby reconciled cash flow to the final change in the cash balance per the balance sheet.

Personally, I like to know what amount of cash would be provided by operations if receivables, payables, and inventory weren't fluctuating all over the place. I then like to be able to easily spot those Balance Sheet accounts whose changes have caused the major deviations in cash flow in order to determine their causes and significance.

While I don't have any actual statistics on the frequency of usage of the two formats, from my own experience I would venture the opinion that the former is easily the most widely used presentation.

USING THE STATEMENT OF CASH FLOWS

The Statement of Cash Flows can be either effective or dangerous as a tool of financial analysis. Some analysts will focus only on the bottom line number, citing the net change in cash to support the position that a company's cash flow is strong or weak. To be meaningful, however, cash flow analysis should also focus on the individual components of cash flow.

I recall one analyst who was impressed by a large positive cash flow that was caused by a company's sales declining precipitously, resulting in little being generated by way of new accounts receivable to replace receivables that were being collected. While the resulting reduction in receivables made bottom line cash flow look very strong, the loss of business was clearly not a sustainable source of cash flow. Analysts who focus only on net cash flow also overlook increases in accounts payable and accrued expenses, which are also not sustainable as sources of cash. Suppliers will either demand payment more promptly at some point in time or go out of business due to cash flow problems of their own.

Conversely, increases in accounts receivable or decreases in accounts payable and accrued expenses, though they may adversely affect cash flow, are certainly not necessarily unhealthy signs in a business. The main concern of cash flow analysis should be that a company not tie up its funds in assets that are failing to generate sufficient cash for the company to meet its obligations and take advantage of future opportunities. For this purpose, cash flow should be analyzed over several years and in detail.

Rapid growth also tends to consume cash and make net cash flow look weaker than it would otherwise. Cash must be paid out for at least that part of plant, equipment, and inventory that is not financed. Rapid growth requires greater outlays for these assets in order to provide for an increasing level of sales, but the assets do not generate cash until sales are booked and accounts receivable collected. The gap between the higher level of cash outlays and the higher level of collections can easily result in negative cash flow during the period of accelerated growth.

Chapter Seven

Following a Transaction through the Financial Statements

We have examined the purpose and uses of financial statements as well as their key features. We will now proceed to focus on important accounting issues and rules that give additional meaning to the numbers. We will also study the use of financial information in more detail. We will begin in this chapter by taking a look at the effects of routine business operations on the financial statements.

To illustrate more clearly how normal business operations affect cash and related accounts, the charts in Exhibit 7–1 demonstrate how a typical transaction of the Hypothetical Company affects its income, Balance Sheet, and cash flow over an operating cycle.

Prior to the transaction, the company's Balance Sheet is liquid, with $600,000 in current assets compared to $100,000 in current liabilities for a current ratio of six to one. It is also lightly leveraged with only $300,000 in total liabilities compared to $500,000 in owners' equity.

THE INVENTORY PURCHASE

The company then purchases $400,000 in inventory with payment due in 30 days. It needs a source of cash equal to the $400,000 use in order for the Balance Sheet to balance.

The Inventory Purchase

EXHIBIT 7–1
Following Cash through the Balance Sheet (the Hypothetical Company)

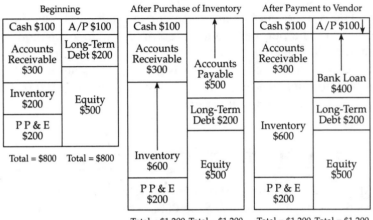

Beginning		After Purchase of Inventory		After Payment to Vendor	
Cash $100	A/P $100	Cash $100		Cash $100	A/P $100
Accounts Receivable $300	Long-Term Debt $200	Accounts Receivable $300	Accounts Payable $500	Accounts Receivable $300	Bank Loan $400
Inventory $200	Equity $500		Long-Term Debt $200	Inventory $600	Long-Term Debt $200
P P & E $200		Inventory $600	Equity $500	P P & E $200	Equity $500
		P P & E $200			
Total = $800	Total = $800	Total = $1,200	Total = $1,200	Total = $1,200	Total = $1,200

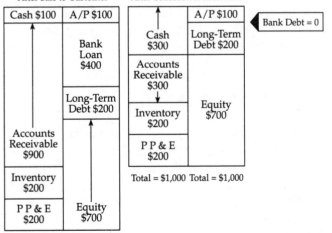

After Sale to Customer		After Collection of Receivable	
Cash $100	A/P $100		A/P $100
	Bank Loan $400	Cash $300	Long-Term Debt $200
	Long-Term Debt $200	Accounts Receivable $300	
Accounts Receivable $900		Inventory $200	Equity $700
Inventory $200		P P & E $200	
P P & E $200	Equity $700		
Total = $1,400	Total = $1,400	Total = $1,000	Total = $1,000

Bank Debt = 0

While part of this could come from collection of accounts receivable, a reduction of cash balances, or bank borrowing, we have assumed that the entire purchase is financed through accounts payable to the vendor.

The ratio of current assets to current liabilities is two to one after the purchase, and inventory, which is less liquid than cash or accounts receivable, is now a far larger portion of current assets. The company is therefore less liquid. With total liabilities of $700,000 compared to equity of $500,000, it is also more highly leveraged.

PAYMENT FOR THE INVENTORY

At the end of 30 days the company pays the vendor, reducing accounts payable back to $100,000. (This would not be the same $100,000 it started with as that balance would have been paid and new amounts added.) Because the reduction in payables was a use of cash, we need an offsetting source to stay in balance. In our example, the $400,000 was borrowed from the company's bank. The company's Balance Sheet is basically unchanged, as one form of short-term debt has been substituted for another.

SALE OF THE INVENTORY

Thirty days after payment to the vendor, the company sells the $400,000 in inventory for $600,000. The $200,000 profit causes an increase in owners' equity from $500,000 to $700,000, but no cash has been received at this point. The entire $600,000 from the sale is therefore recorded as an increase in accounts receivable.

The $200,000 source of cash from the increase in equity plus the $400,000 from the reduction in inventory is equal to the $600,000 increase in accounts receivable, a use of cash. No net cash is therefore provided, and bank debt stays at $400,000. The company's liquidity has improved with the large increase in receivables and more modest reduction in inventory. The current ratio is now greater than two to one, and total liabilities equal owners' equity. The company is still more highly leveraged than before the transaction due to the new debt that cannot yet be repaid.

COLLECTION OF
ACCOUNT RECEIVABLE

Thirty days after the sale, however, the company collects the account receivable. The $600,000 reduction in the receivable is a source of cash. However, $400,000 of this is used to pay off bank debt. The remaining $200,000, in our example, is added to cash. (It could have been used to pay off accounts payable and long-term debt or to make some reduction in one or both of these accounts, with the balance added to cash.) Equity is unchanged at $700,000, as no new income is generated as a result of collection of accounts that generated the previously recognized income.

The company is extremely liquid, with a current ratio of eight to one and most of its current assets in cash and receivables. Leverage is at its low point, with only $300,000 in liabilities compared to $700,000 in equity. While this transaction therefore caused the company to become temporarily less liquid and more leveraged, ultimately the profits and collection of receivables improved its financial condition. For an overview of the cash cycle, see Exhibit 7–2.

This example shows the effects of a transaction over a short period of time on a business that is otherwise stagnant. In Chapter Twelve, we will see how growth or decline in the company's business, as well as its efficiency and profitability, can change the impact on its Balance Sheet and cash flow.

EXHIBIT 7–2
The Cash Cycle

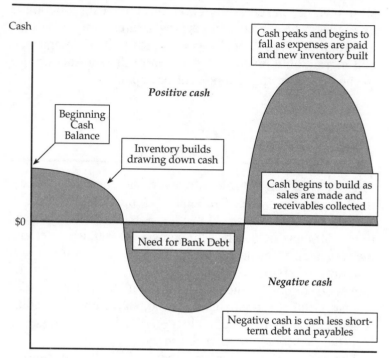

Cash

Cash peaks and begins to fall as expenses are paid and new inventory built

Positive cash

Beginning Cash Balance

Inventory builds drawing down cash

Cash begins to build as sales are made and receivables collected

$0

Need for Bank Debt

Negative cash

Negative cash is cash less short-term debt and payables

Time

Chapter Eight

Special Inventory Valuation and Depreciation Reporting Issues

The rules for reporting most financial statement accounts are somewhat standardized so that the reader may be reasonably assured that what the numbers show is a fair representation of what is actually happening. Standardization is also necessary in order to compare one company's financial strength and performance to that of its peers.

Nevertheless, accounting standards permit some choices between alternate methods of reporting. Fortunately, the financial report must disclose to the reader, by way of footnotes to the financial statements, which of several equally acceptable accounting methods has been selected. (We discuss financial statement footnotes in some detail in Chapter Eleven.)

Two of the areas offering considerable latitude in the manner of presentation are inventory valuation and the depreciation of property, plant, and equipment. Since these items appear routinely on most companies' financial statements, they warrant special attention.

INVENTORY VALUATION
ALTERNATIVES

The valuation of inventory would be quite simple and rational if each item could be valued according to its own specifically identified cost, and indeed this *specific identification* method is used in instances where a relatively low volume of high-priced and clearly differentiable items can be tracked. Automobiles and boats sold at retail are common examples of specific identification, as are houses.

Most products, however, are purchased in large lots of standardized product at a given cost per unit for each lot. These products do not lend themselves easily to specific identification. It would not be practical, for example, for The Easy Company to track each toothpick separately through the production and shipping processes for valuation purposes. Instead, all units purchased in each lot receive the same value, which is equal to the total purchase price of the lot divided by the number of units purchased. (Other manufacturing costs are also added to the cost of purchases, but for simplification we will use purchases as the total cost of goods sold in our discussion.)

The choice among alternate accounting treatments lies in the identification of which units are assumed to have been sold versus which remain in inventory at the end of the period. The method selected will influence the ending inventory value as well as the cost of goods sold. It will thereby also influence net income, total asset value and owners' equity. For illustration, assume all goods are purchased in five lots as follows:

Purchases for Year

Lot	Units	Cost per Unit	Total Cost
1	2,000	$8	$ 16,000
2	1,000	9	9,000

Lot	Units	Cost per Unit	Total Cost
3	3,000	10	30,000
4	2,000	10	20,000
5	3,000	12	36,000
	11,000		$111,000

Assume that a total of 9,000 units are sold during the year. The choices are whether to assume these sales consisted of the first 9,000 units purchased, the last 9,000 units purchased, or the average cost of all units purchased during the period. These alternatives are called first-in-first-out or FIFO, last-in-first-out or LIFO, and average cost respectively. See Exhibit 8–1 on the following page.

Some really droll financial types even came up with an acronym for inventory that the firm gets stuck with because it doesn't sell. It's called FIST, or first-in-still-there. Take a minute to get control of your convulsive laughter and wipe the tears from your eyes so that we can continue.

If the 9,000 units are allocated to cost of goods sold based on FIFO or LIFO, the cost will be:

	FIFO				LIFO		
Lot	Units	Cost per Unit	Total Cost	Lot	Units	Cost per Unit	Total Cost
1	2,000	8	$16,000	5	3,000	12	$36,000
2	1,000	9	9,000	4	2,000	10	20,000
3	3,000	10	30,000	3	3,000	10	30,000
4	2,000	10	20,000	2	1,000	9	9,000
5	1,000	12	12,000				
	9,000		$87,000		9,000		$95,000

Based on the average cost, the cost of goods sold would be:

$111,000/11,000 units = $10.10 per unit

9,000 × $10.10 = $90,900

EXHIBIT 8–1
Inventory Choices

The ending inventory in each of these scenarios is the total cost of all the purchases (goods available for sale) less the cost of goods sold:

	FIFO	*LIFO*	*Average Cost*
Cost of goods purchased	$111,000	$111,000	$111,000
Cost of goods sold	87,000	95,000	90,900
Ending inventory	$ 24,000	$ 16,000	$ 20,100

RELATIVE MERITS OF FIFO, LIFO, AND AVERAGE COST

There is a certain intuitive logic behind the notion that the first unit purchased is the first unit sold (FIFO). It just seems to be the natural order of things. The principal objection to this method is that it does not match the cost of units being sold with the cost of replacing those units in an environment where significant price changes are taking place. It does, however, value the remaining inventory, the latest units purchased, at the approximate current cost of replacing that inventory.

LIFO, on the other hand, values the cost of units sold at prices close to their current replacement costs. Since the ending inventory may consist of units purchased some time ago, however, its value in the financial statements may differ considerably from current market costs.

The average cost method combines the best and the worst of FIFO and LIFO in a sort of compromise. It involves a slightly more complicated calculation but is ideal for those who can't make up their minds between FIFO and LIFO. Since accounting is not politics, however, the average cost compromise is not as commonly chosen as FIFO or LIFO.

Tax consequences can play an important role in the selection of an inventory valuation policy. During periods of rising prices, for example, FIFO will match inventory purchased at lower prices in earlier periods against sales in the current period, resulting in higher reported profits and therefore higher taxes. For this reason, LIFO tends to be more popular during inflationary periods.

In reading financial statements, it is important to know which method of inventory valuation has been used. One must consider the likely effects of this selection on Balance Sheet and Income Statement results given trends in prices. The method of valuation should be disclosed in the footnotes following the financial statements, and often the impact on inventory values of using another method will also be disclosed. The reader can easily determine the impact on cost of goods sold and net profits by substituting the alternate figures for beginning and ending inventory in the cost of goods sold calculation.

DEPRECIATION ISSUES

Selection of the method of depreciation for long-lived assets presents two problems: What is the useful life of the asset, and in what increments does its value diminish over this period? In order to understand the significance of these questions, it is useful to reexamine the purpose of depreciation.

Depreciation allocates the cost of an asset over its useful life in order to match this cost against the revenues produced by the asset. To do this, the total cost of the asset is divided among the number of periods it will be used. Clearly we must estimate the useful life of the asset at the time of purchase, since the depreciation charges must begin in the first period of usage and cannot await the final disposition of the asset for determination of what its useful life will be.

Useful Life of Assets

The projection of useful life is complicated by the fact that there is more than one factor that will enter into its calculation. There is, for example, the amount of time the asset can be expected to be physically operative at its estimated level of usage before the cost of repairing it is no longer cost effective vis-à-vis the cost of replacing it. That could be termed the *physical* life of the asset. While its calculation would be relatively straightforward, it nevertheless involves estimates of the level of production, durability of the asset, future repair costs, and replacement costs.

An increasingly important and far more difficult estimate in the useful life calculation, however, must take into account *obsolescence.* How long can a piece of equipment operate economically before a new and technologically superior piece of equipment can do the same thing so much more efficiently that the company cannot compete in its industry using the old equipment? At this time, the equipment's useful life has ended even though it may be physically capable of production for a considerably longer period. So you can see that the determination of useful life involves a lot of guess work, which, in finance, we call estimating. As a rule of thumb, equipment generally has a useful life of five to seven years. It could be more or less, however, given special characteristics of the industry or the equipment.

If a company is too optimistic in its assessment of the useful life of its equipment, it will end up taking losses on the sale or retirement of the equipment. That is to say, the equipment will become useless while it still shows a value on the Balance Sheet. That value must be fully or partially removed through a charge against income in the period in which it is determined that the equipment is worthless or of lesser value than stated.

In recent years, many companies have announced massive write-down and write-off charges against income, caused, at least in part, by this type of accounting adjustment. Few things in the world of accounting are more exciting than a massive write down.

If a company is not optimistic enough about the useful life of its equipment, it will end up generating revenue and income from this equipment for some time after the equipment has been fully depreciated. That is to say, there will be no value for the equipment stated on the Balance Sheet and no cost of depreciation charged against the revenues produced during the remaining period of service of the equipment. Note that the company's income is overstated during this period by the lack of any charges for the use of its equipment, just as it was understated during the earlier periods by charging too much of the cost of the equipment against these periods of service.

Buildings generally have a useful life of 20 to 30 years for depreciation purposes, though many financial analysts contend that they do not really depreciate at all and therefore have an infinite useful life. These are the same folks who say that real estate always goes up in value. *Appreciation* cannot be shown in the financial statements, since that would not be conservative and would cause income to be recognized before it is realized.[1] The real estate boosters must therefore settle for the argument that showing depreciation for buildings merely shows a cost where in fact there is none. They have no problem with adding depreciation of buildings back into income to get what they consider to be a true measure of income. Usually, in fact, they just add all depreciation back on the presumption that most of it is buildings and, in any case, they don't want to mess with sorting it all out. Today, however, there are fewer of these people than there were a few years ago.

It is true enough that buildings may deteriorate physically at a less rapid rate than the 20 or 30 years used in financial statements. What is now more commonly recognized, however, is that, in an era of rapid global changes in the economics of production, distribution, and communications technology, buildings can become economically obsolete. Geographic areas deteriorate or become less competitive. Space requirements dictate different design layouts. Overall demand for certain kinds of buildings falls. These factors influence values and suggest that depreciation of buildings is appropriate and that the useful life determination must consider some of the same factors used for other types of assets.

Land is different. There is simply no physical deterioration in land, and it doesn't become obsolete by means of the discovery of a technologically superior type of land. While it may decline in value due to demographics or general economic trends, the direction of any change in value is largely a matter of speculation. Land is therefore not subject

---

[1] Accounting rules require that revenue be "realized" through a cash transaction or obligation before it can be recognized for reporting purposes.

to periodic depreciation for financial reporting purposes. However, if a company becomes aware of a material decline in the value of land carried on its Balance Sheet for any reason, it should reduce the stated cost or value to current market value.

Straight-Line versus Accelerated Depreciation

The other depreciation issue to be resolved is, given the estimate of useful life, how should the total depreciation (the total cost of the asset) be allocated to each of these periods? At first glance one would be inclined to say, "Why not equally?" If an asset costs $100,000 and has a useful life of 10 years, wouldn't $10,000 of the asset be used each year?

In many cases, this is a reasonable approach. It is widely used under the name *straight-line* depreciation. The periodic amount of depreciation is equal to the initial cost of the asset divided by the number of periods of its useful life. Were one to draw a graph of the periodic charges over time, it would appear as a perfectly horizontal straight line. Were one to graph the decline in the value of the asset over a period of time, it would appear as a declining straight line. The rationale for calling this form of depreciation straight-line depreciation is therefore unimpeachable.

Most other forms of depreciation can be lumped into a single category called *accelerated* depreciation. They share the common assumption that depreciable property and equipment loses more of its value in its early years of deployment than toward the end of its life. For a personal analogy, you probably know that the day you drive your new car off the lot it becomes a used car and absorbs a precipitous drop in value. Accelerated depreciation doesn't work quite as abruptly, but it's that kind of a thing.

The following table illustrates the effects of accelerated depreciation on property with a five-year useful life. The accompanying graph (see Exhibit 8–2) shows how the value

EXHIBIT 8–2
Straight-Line versus Accelerated Depreciation—How Net Asset Value Declines over Time

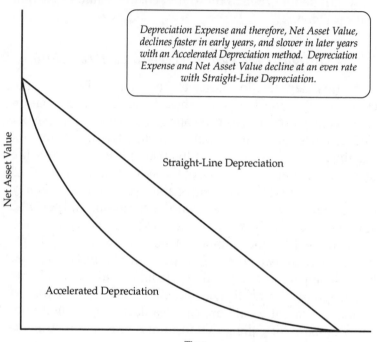

Depreciation Expense and therefore, Net Asset Value, declines faster in early years, and slower in later years with an Accelerated Depreciation method. Depreciation Expense and Net Asset Value decline at an even rate with Straight-Line Depreciation.

Straight-Line Depreciation

Accelerated Depreciation

Net Asset Value

Time

of an asset changes under accelerated depreciation compared to straight-line depreciation.

Year	Depreciation	Asset Value
0		$100,000
1	$33,333	66,667
2	26,667	40,000
3	20,000	20,000
4	13,333	6,667
5	6,667	0

Accelerated depreciation increases costs in the early years of equipment usage and decreases them in later years.

It therefore tends to penalize income in the early years and augment it in later years. It seems most appropriate where technological obsolescence is a concern, as it more quickly reduces the value of the asset over its estimated useful life. Since accelerated depreciation also tends to reduce reported net income in the early periods following asset purchases, it is also popular for tax purposes. Since a company is not required to use the same method of reporting for tax purposes as it uses for financial reporting purposes, it may well use straight-line for financial reporting and an accelerated method, known as the accelerated cost recovery system (ACRS), for income tax reporting.

Taxes that are shown as an expense for financial reporting but are not payable due to the lesser income reported for income tax reporting are shown on the Balance Sheet as "deferred taxes." The accounting presumption is that these taxes will have to be paid at some future date when accelerated depreciation results in lower depreciation charges than straight-line. That would produce higher income tax payments to the government relative to income tax expense for financial reporting purposes. When this reversal takes place depends on how rapidly the company continues to acquire new assets.

Clearly the estimate of useful life, combined with the choice of straight-line or accelerated depreciation, can have a considerable effect on the asset values and reported income of a company. It is the responsibility of management and its independent auditors to select methods of depreciation and to estimate useful lives on a basis that is reasonable, and to that end the ACRS guidelines are available through the Internal Revenue Service and are observed by the accounting profession at least for income tax reporting and often for financial reporting as well. It is your responsibility as a user of financial statements to understand the alternatives and their effects on reported income and the Balance Sheet.

Chapter Nine

Intangible Assets and Amortization

AMORTIZATION

Until now, depreciation has occupied a unique position in our discussions as a direct noncash charge against income that needs to be added back as the first step in deriving cash flow. In point of fact, however, there is another expense that has similar characteristics in terms of its accounting treatment and its effects on cash flow. That expense is called *amortization,* and it has been assuming an increasingly important role in financial reporting. While depreciation reflects the periodic allocation of the costs of acquiring *tangible* assets such as real property and equipment, amortization reflects the periodic allocation of the costs of acquiring or developing *intangible* assets.

INTANGIBLE ASSETS

Intangible assets are those that we can't feel or see but that nevertheless have considerable value in generating revenues. Among the most common types of intangible assets are patents, trademarks, copyrights, and franchises. Bugs Bunny and Donald Duck are prominent examples of intangible assets, and are certainly among the author's favorites. The rights to a book, a song, or a movie script are considered intellectual property, as opposed to real property, and are therefore intangible assets.

In today's high-tech environment, patent rights for everything from new drugs to new microchip technology have become critical assets, often resulting in litigation to determine whether one company's new product violates another company's patents. The fortunes of companies like Intel and Advanced Micro Devices depend heavily on their continuing disputes over patent protection and violation.

When Intel comes out with a new chip, Advanced Micro usually comes out with a virtually identical kind of chip and gets sued by Intel. Billions of dollars are at stake in their continuous rounds of litigation over what can be patented and what constitutes a violation of that patent.

Important brand names, such as Coca-Cola, are similarly protected from unauthorized use through trademarks. A McDonald's franchise has a value far beyond that of its equipment, furnishings, and food inventory. That extraordinary value is the intangible value of the franchise itself.

These assets may not even be shown on the Balance Sheet, and, if they are shown, they are shown at the cost of their acquisition or development. Their value may therefore be significantly understated.

GOODWILL

Some intangible assets are lumped into a general category called *goodwill*. Goodwill frequently arises when one company buys another for a price in excess of the acquired company's net asset value (owners' equity) at the time of acquisition. The difference between the purchase price and the net asset value is deemed to have real value to the buyer. When this value cannot be allocated to specific assets, it is called goodwill or, more descriptively, "purchase price in excess of net assets of companies acquired."

What is common to all of these examples of intangible assets is that there is something that you just can't get your hands on that nevertheless may generate huge amounts of revenue. If this asset has a finite life, its cost to the company should be amortized over that life if it is shown on the Balance Sheet.

It should be noted that some companies maintain that certain intangible assets maintain their value indefinitely and therefore choose not to amortize them. Whether that position is supportable is a matter of management judgment, auditor review, and the scrutiny of the financial community (soon to include you).

Intangible assets are created in many other instances in which companies spend material sums of money that are expected to generate substantial revenues in future reporting periods. These might include expenditures for advertising or research and development. We will look at two examples that are prevalent in their respective industries: *unamortized film costs* in the entertainment business and *premium acquisition costs* in the insurance business.

AMORTIZATION OF MOTION PICTURE FILM COSTS

The costs of producing a major motion picture consist largely of payments for the services of actors, directors, and technicians who work on the film. Additional expenses include payments to acquire intellectual property such as the screen-rights to a best-selling novel or a screenplay. Wardrobes, props, equipment and facility rentals, transportation costs, and a host of other costs also make up the cost of the film.

These costs do not result in the acquisition of property or equipment subject to depreciation. Most of what real assets may be acquired for the film do not have a useful life beyond the period during which the film is produced. The film may take years to complete and, in any case, can only be expected to generate a small portion of its theatrical revenues during the accounting period in which it is completed. Much of its theatrical (box office) revenue and virtually all of its home video, foreign, cable, and television revenues can be expected to be earned in subsequent periods.

It therefore makes no sense to expense these costs as they are incurred. To do so would result in enormous costs and no revenues during production and revenues without any matching costs in subsequent periods. These costs are therefore accumulated as an asset called unamortized film costs until the film is released and begins to generate revenues.

Now things get tricky. The costs will be amortized over the period of revenue receipt through a noncash charge called *amortization of film costs*. If you thought there were problems in estimating the useful life of a depreciable asset, think about how you would go about estimating the useful life of a movie that is just being released for theatrical distribution. Also, given an estimate of its useful life, which is the period during which it can be expected to generate meaningful revenue, how much of the cost would you allocate to each period?

While we know that most of the revenues will be generated during the earliest periods of release, a formula such as the one used for accelerated depreciation will not do. The timing of revenue receipts is too erratic and unpredictable. So the film industry has come up with what is called the *individual film forecast* method of allocating the costs of the film.

It works like this. For each film the company estimates the total revenues it will generate as well as the timing and source of these revenues. Based on all available information relative to how well the film will be received, the company projects the level of box office revenues. Based on the performance of similar types of movies, it then projects the timing of these receipts. It then does the same for home video, foreign, cable, and television.

The result is a pattern of revenue receipt against which the amortization of costs can be matched. If 50 percent of total revenues are expected to be received in the first year of release, then 50 percent of costs will be written off in the first year. Costs are then allocated to each subsequent year in proportion to the revenues expected to be received in those years. It is fairly common for about 80 percent of the film's cost to be written off in the first three years.

Sound a little crazy? Carrying this estimating stuff too far? Well, how else would you do it? Film companies are pretty good at determining how well a certain type of film will do in foreign markets versus domestic, how much its theatrical revenues will decline from the first week of its release during each subsequent week, and what this kind of film can be expected to do in the home video, cable, and TV markets relative to its domestic box office. All of this is based on patterns experienced with other films, perhaps tempered by a bit of judgment.

The hard part is figuring out the amount of total revenues to be allocated. Who really knows how successful a film will be until it is released? A bit of limited testing through select audience responses may provide a clue, but it is also important to make the appropriate adjustments to the forecast following the first few days of domestic box office release. Fortunately, for financial reporting purposes, the adjustments can be made any time between the release of the film and the end of the accounting period.

INSURANCE COMPANIES AND POLICY ACQUISITION COSTS

Compared to Hollywood's problems, the insurance industry's policy acquisition costs treatment seems trivial. Policy acquisition costs is the industry's name for the costs of selling insurance policies. Why not just treat them as an expense in the period during which they are incurred? The industry has developed statistics that show that a certain percentage of policies will be renewed in subsequent periods with little or no additional cost or effort on their part. An analogy can be made to magazine subscriptions, for which a certain portion of the cost of selling the subscription may be allocated to projected renewals in future periods.

The costs of paying insurance salespersons and direct mail or newspaper advertising is therefore seen as an asset that will generate future revenues. These costs must be amortized over the period during which they are expected to generate the related premiums as *amortization of policy acquisition costs.*

While a film company's unamortized film costs can represent a large amount relative to its total assets, that should not normally be the case for an insurance company's policy acquisition costs. That is because a larger portion of a film company's total assets is the cost of making films, while insurance companies' liquid assets for servicing its clients and paying claims should be far more substantial in relation to marketing costs that it feels will benefit future periods.

Continental Corporation and Primerica, for example, reported deferred policy acquisition costs in 1992 equal to 3.6 percent and 25.8 percent of assets employed in insurance operations respectively. Generally insurance companies' deferred policy acquisition costs fall somewhere within this range. A filmed entertainment company, on the other hand, might have unamortized film costs easily in excess of 60 percent of total assets employed in its film business.

As an emerging financial analyst, beware of unamortized costs that seem way out of proportion to revenues being generated. It may be that the company is reluctant to recognize that its expenditures are not generating the expected revenues because it doesn't want to have to take a charge to current income.

Chapter Ten

Service Companies

Service companies have been assuming an increasingly important role in our economy. Their accounting practices can be more varied and innovative than those of product- or merchandise-oriented companies, reflecting the diverse nature of their operations. They generate revenues by providing services instead of selling products and as a result show neither inventory nor costs of goods sold on their financial statements. Instead of costs of goods sold, service companies simply show the costs of services provided. The major difference is that this presentation does not involve adjusting for beginning and ending inventory.

There may, however, be differences in timing between when the cost of providing a service is incurred and when revenue for the service can be recognized. These differences can be reconciled by *capitalizing* costs as assets on the Balance Sheet and amortizing them over future periods, as in the case of the policy acquisition costs of our insurance company.

Exhibit 10–1 contains the financial statements of Bell-South, a regional telephone operating company expanding into global telecommunications, which not only provides an example of how such statements might differ from those of a production or distribution company but also provides an excellent example of a company's efforts to simplify and explain its statements for the reader.

Examples of service companies include public utilities, financial service companies, laundries, airlines, data pro-

EXHIBIT 10-1

Condensed Consolidated Statements of

INCOME

BELLSOUTH CORPORATION

These statements are a summary of the company's operating performance for specific annual periods. They show revenues and expenses that result in net income. Revenues are from the sale of services and products to BellSouth customers. Operating expenses include costs of services and products; depreciation; and selling, general and administrative expenses. Taxes also are a major expense category.

Interstate access – These revenues are related to connecting long distance calls across state lines for our customers. Measured in minutes, there was the equivalent of nearly 263 *years* worth of these calls *every day* in 1992.

Total operating revenues – Total operating revenues reached a record in 1992, exceeding $15 billion for the first time.

	For the years ended December 31,		
(In millions)	1992	1991	1990
Operating revenues:			
Network and related services			
Local service	$ 6,236.0	$ 5,846.2	$ 5,664.6
Interstate access	2,945.6	2,858.1	2,841.9
Intrastate access	871.8	866.7	911.8
Toll	1,248.8	1,373.7	1,565.4
Directory advertising and publishing	1,459.8	1,426.3	1,394.2
Wireless communications	1,195.6	774.5	557.3
Other services	1,244.0	1,300.0	1,410.2
Total operating revenues	$15,201.6	$14,445.5	$14,345.4
Operating expenses	$12,040.9	$11,635.8	$11,318.7
Operating income	3,160.7	2,809.7	3,026.7
Interest expense	746.4	802.1	774.3
Other income, net	177.6	252.7	156.8
Income before income taxes, extraordinary loss and cumulative effect of change in method of accounting	2,591.9	2,260.3	2,409.2
Provision for income taxes	933.5	753.4	777.7
Income before extraordinary loss and cumulative effect of change in method of accounting	1,658.4	1,506.9	1,631.5
Extraordinary loss, net of tax	(40.7)	–	–
Cumulative effect of change in method of accounting, net of tax	–	(35.4)	–
Net income	$ 1,617.7	$ 1,471.5	$ 1,631.5

Wireless communications – Worldwide revenues from cellular and paging increased more than 54 percent in 1992, as BellSouth surpassed the 1 million mark in cellular phone customers.

Operating income – Operating income increased 12.5 percent in 1992, as a result of revenues growing at a faster rate, 5.2 percent, than expenses, which increased 3.5 percent.

Extraordinary loss – This one-time charge resulted from refinancing $550 million in bonds, which will save nearly $400 million in interest expense over the lives of the new debt issues.

Net income – "The bottom line" increased 9.9 percent in 1992, rebounding from a 9.8 percent decline in the prior year.

EXHIBIT 10–1 (*continued*)

Condensed Consolidated

BALANCE SHEETS

BELLSOUTH CORPORATION

The balance sheet is considered a "snapshot" of the company's financial position at the end of the year. Assets are economic resources that are expected to benefit future business activities. Liabilities are claims against those assets, or money that BellSouth owes.

	December 31, 1992	1991
(*In millions*)		
Assets:		
Current assets	$ 3,671.0	$ 3,637.5
Property, plant and equipment, net	24,272.6	24,058.5
Investments and advances, intangible assets, and deferred charges and other assets	3,519.1	3,245.7
Total assets	$31,462.7	$30,941.7
Liabilities and Shareholders' Equity:		
Current liabilities	$ 5,022.2	$ 4,911.2
Long-term debt	7,359.7	7,676.9
Deferred credits and other liabilities	5,282.2	5,248.7
Shareholders' equity	13,798.6	13,104.9
Total liabilities and shareholders' equity	$31,462.7	$30,941.7

Current assets – Among the assets whose amounts are included here are cash, receivables (net of those estimated to be uncollectible) and materials and supplies.

Property, plant and equipment, net – The majority of BellSouth's total assets historically is represented by the "fixed assets" that make up and maintain the telecommunications infrastructure, such as fiber optic cable, switches and cellular towers.

Long-term debt – The amount of debt maturing after one year declined $317.2 million in 1992. This helped BellSouth's overall debt ratio improve to 39.0 percent in 1992 from 41.3 percent the year before.

Shareholders' equity – Sometimes called "net worth" or "book value," this number equals assets minus liabilities, and represents our shareholders' ownership in BellSouth.

EXHIBIT 10–1 (*concluded*)

Condensed Consolidated Statements of
CASH FLOWS

BELLSOUTH CORPORATION

These statements reconcile the changes in "cash and cash equivalents" from the end of one year to the end of the following year. Cash and cash equivalents is included in Current Assets on the Balance Sheets (page 29).

(In millions)	For the years ended December 31,		
	1992	1991	1990
Net income	$ 1,617.7	$ 1,471.5	$ 1,631.5
Adjustments to net income, primarily depreciation	3,470.1	2,985.9	3,014.8
Changes in operating assets and liabilities	(141.0)	(67.5)	(119.8)
Cash provided by operating activities	4,946.8	4,389.9	4,526.5
Cash used for investing activities	(3,591.8)	(3,776.4)	(3,054.8)
Cash used for financing activities	(1,416.8)	(576.8)	(1,473.8)
Increase (decrease) in cash and cash equivalents	(61.8)	36.7	(2.1)
Beginning cash and cash equivalents	327.3	290.6	292.7
Ending cash and cash equivalents	$ 265.5	$ 327.3	$ 290.6

Adjustments, primarily depreciation – A portion of the original cost of assets that will be in use for several years, such as plant and equipment, is charged to operating expenses every year as depreciation (see Condensed Statements of Income, page 28). Because depreciation is a non-cash expense, it is recognized as a positive adjustment to net income.

Investing activities – This figure is shown because these activities represent cash BellSouth spent to invest in assets. Capital expenditures to modernize the telephone network are the largest item in this category.

Financing activities – Cash dividends paid to shareholders (nearly $1.1 billion in 1992) are included in this line as a use of cash.

cessing companies, cable television providers, travel agents, law firms, accounting offices, advertising agencies, hospitals, hotels, and a host of others that we encounter regularly in our daily lives but are too numerous to mention.

FINANCIAL SERVICES COMPANIES

The financial statements of service companies not only differ from those of companies that manufacture and sell products, but they also differ considerably among one another depending on the type of service provided and the operating characteristics of the industry. Financial services companies, for example, generally show large amounts of dollar-denominated loans and investments on their Balance Sheets and relatively little owners' equity. Less equity is thought to be needed due to the certainty with which they can value their assets and their confidence in their ability to realize these values.

Various types of financial service companies, however, have their own particular structures. Banks, for example, have traditionally taken in deposits and have used these deposits to finance their extension of loans. Their assets therefore largely consist of loans and their liabilities largely of deposits. Historically, most of their income has come from interest earned, and most of their expense has been interest paid. Owners' equity may be only around 6 percent of assets, since most assets have a fixed dollar value and are considered highly prudent and therefore collectible.

The banking industry is currently undergoing change, and banks' financial statements are beginning to reflect both more diversity and more equity. This trend has been driven largely by competition among financial service companies to make greater inroads into what were once traditionally separate markets of one or the other type of institution. To the extent that this trend continues, the banks' financial statements will continue to change to reflect their new lines of business and new perceptions of risk.

The assets of insurance companies largely reflect the various investments they feel will generate the income and offer the liquidity they will need to fund policy claims. These objectives generally call for a heavy emphasis on marketable securities consisting of notes and bonds of various maturities as well as common and preferred stocks, but insurance companies may also invest to a lesser extent in real estate.

The liabilities of insurance companies are heavily weighted by the various reserves and liabilities for the payment of claims that have been made or that statistics suggest will be made at some future time. Revenues are derived from policy premiums earned and from investments. Expenses are mostly actual and projected policy claims.

Securities brokerage firms have a great deal of their assets, as one might expect, in securities. These may be held for their own account, in which case they are investment securities, or for meeting the demands of customers, in which case they are trading securities. Funds due from other brokers and from clients are also significant. Liabilities may consist of various short-term financing arrangements used to carry the securities held as assets as well as funds due to brokers and clients. Revenues consist of commissions on securities trades, perhaps fees from investment banking activities, and any profits from trading securities for the firm's own account. Commissions paid to brokers are a rather large expense for securities firms.

CAPITAL-INTENSIVE
SERVICE COMPANIES

Another category of services companies might best be described as *capital intensive,* which is to say that revenues are largely derived from the use of property, plant, and equipment. Among the industries fitting this description would be public utilities, airlines and other transportation companies, cable television companies, data processing companies, hospitals, and hotels. The Balance Sheets of these types of companies reflect their heavy investment in the property and equipment that generates their revenues. They therefore reflect substantial noncurrent assets and usually heavy debt or lease obligations with which these assets were financed. Some, such as public utilities, may reflect surprisingly little liquidity, since they are by and large cash (as opposed to credit) businesses and their predictable cash flow from operations provides the liquidity they need.

The expenses of capital-intensive companies can be expected to reflect the heavy depreciation of their substantial noncurrent assets. Profitability may be fairly steady, as in the case of utilities, or cyclical (i.e., erratic), as in the case of airlines.

PEOPLE-INTENSIVE SERVICE COMPANIES

A third type of service company, which can be expected to show still different financial characteristics, provides professional services in a manner that is *people intensive*. Examples include law firms, accounting service providers, ad agencies, architectural service companies, employment and temporary help agencies, and management consulting firms. These are the companies whose assets "walk out the door every night."

Since these walking assets generate revenues, however, the Balance Sheets of their companies largely reflect the accounts receivable they generate. The receivables are especially prominent because of the lack of any inventory or significant amount of noncurrent assets such as plant and equipment.

The greatest expense of the people companies is, of course, their payroll. They usually have a modest amount of debt since their lack of inventory and heavy equipment eliminates both the need and the collateral to borrow.

Service companies represent the fastest-growing segment of the economy. In terms of accounting and reporting, they seem to offer more variety and more challenges than the traditional manufacturing, wholesale, or retail companies. But then even tradition isn't what it used to be.

Chapter Eleven

What Are the Rules that Preparers of Financial Statements Must Play By?

You probably think of financial statement preparers as a bunch of wild and crazy guys who can do whatever they want with the numbers. That's not correct. A lot of them are women, and they are subject to an elaborate set of rules that have been developed and refined over the years to assure that the reader of statements receives a "fair presentation." These rules are called Generally Accepted Accounting Principles (GAAP).

GAAP AND GAAS

Any financial statement intended for the use of anyone other than the management of the company should be prepared in conformity with GAAP. In addition, the independent outside accountants who audit the statements are required to do so in accordance with Generally Accepted Auditing Standards (GAAS).

The principal requirements for a fair presentation of financial information are that they comply with GAAP and GAAS, that they disclose all information necessary for the reader to fully understand the financial statements, and that the auditors express an *opinion* regarding the financial presentation.

The first rule is therefore that the preparer and the auditors follow the rules. The second, the disclosure requirement, is fulfilled by means of footnotes to the statements, which generally follow the full set of reports. The opinion of the auditors (outside accountants) is contained in an *opinion letter,* which used to precede the financial statements but now often follows the statements and the footnotes.

Accounting and reporting standards outlined under GAAP generally establish specific criteria for critical reporting issues such as when revenue can be recognized (recorded) for financial reporting purposes. Among different industries there may be different criteria for the recognition of revenue, as the operating characteristics of an industry may determine what is feasible or reasonable for that industry.

Within each industry or group of industries with similar operating characteristics, however, revenue recognition is determined according to the same criteria. It is standard practice, for example, for manufacturing and distribution companies to recognize revenue upon shipment and invoicing (billing) the customer. Shipping and billing should therefore occur simultaneously.

Without a common standard, companies might record revenues based on the receipt of orders, the shipment of merchandise, or the receipt of payment. Reported results would simply not be comparable for companies using such dissimilar techniques.

In some of the areas we have previously discussed there is not a single practice but a range of acceptable practices for reporting financial information. In these cases, the financial preparer should select one of the acceptable alternatives and disclose to the reader which of the alternatives has been selected.

DISCLOSURES

The disclosures contained in the footnotes to the financial statements are helpful in understanding a company's accounting practices. These footnotes are usually so instructive that many financial analysts prefer to read them before they read the statements themselves. Some of the disclosures commonly found in footnotes to the financial statements might appear as follows:

General

Outlines the nature of the business or businesses in which the company is engaged and the operating characteristics of these businesses. This brief description is important because it is difficult to understand a company's accounting practices and financial results without understanding the nature of its operations.

Summary of Significant Accounting Policies

Principles of consolidation. What wholly or partially owned companies are included in the statements, and what accounting guidelines have been followed for their inclusion? This is an area where GAAP provides fairly specific guidelines for subsidiaries (companies where ownership is substantial enough for the subject company to exercise control), which ought to be consolidated. Consolidated subsidiaries are those whose financial data are mixed in with the data for the subject, or parent, company instead of showing ownership as a separate net asset and the subsidiary's net profit or loss as a separate Income Statement item.

Revenue recognition. As previously stated, revenue recognition criteria are well prescribed for various types of companies. However, for companies in industries for which the prescribed methods may not be commonly known or that have unique revenue recognition problems, it is a good idea to offer a description of the standards followed by the company in order to facilitate an understanding of the statements.

Treatment of "excess of purchase price over net assets of business acquired." This is where the treatment of what is commonly referred to as *goodwill* is discussed. Whether it is being amortized and, if so, over what period of time is disclosed here.

Property and equipment. Breaks down property and equipment into specific categories. Shows the useful lives and methods of depreciation for each category as well as its accumulated depreciation and net asset value.

Inventory. Tells what method of inventory valuation has been selected (FIFO, LIFO, or average cost). Also may break down components of inventory into raw materials, work in process, and finished goods. The significance of this breakdown will be discussed in Chapter Twelve.

Research and development costs. Tells whether or under what circumstances research and development expenses are capitalized as assets to benefit future periods or charged as expenses of the current period. This is one of the important areas allowing some management discretion. Other things being equal, it is more conservative (offers a less favorable financial picture relative to what is actually happening) to expense R&D even though it may well benefit future periods. Who's to know?

Definition of cash equivalents. Instead of carrying a lot of cash in checking accounts that don't earn any interest, most companies invest in the short-term debt instruments of government, government agencies, and high-quality corporations. These are called *cash equivalents* on the financial statement if they meet certain criteria for easy conversion into cash when cash is needed. These criteria are defined in this section of the footnotes.

Warranties or any other unusual terms of sale. It is important to disclose whether there are any unusual obligations arising from the sale of the company's products or services. Warranties may give rise to significant but unpredictable future expenses or even lead to the cancellation of sales or contracts.

Description of Credit Facilities

What agreements has the company negotiated with its lenders? (How much can it borrow and on what terms?)

Description of Terms and Funding of Employee Benefit and Retirement Plans

Describes who is eligible for benefits, current costs to the company for benefits provided, estimated future costs of providing benefits, and amount of funding provided to meet future costs. This section has recently attracted considerable interest as many companies, under new GAAP rules, have taken heavy charges against current income to provide for deficiencies in funding for future benefits.

Reconciliation of Income Tax Expenses (Provision for Income Taxes) to Statutory Federal and State Tax Rates

If there are timing differences created by the use of one form of accounting for income tax filing and another for financial reporting, or if there are tax credits that reduce its income taxes, the company shows what effects these items have on reported income taxes, on actual amounts due or paid, and on those that would have been required under the prevailing tax rates had not all of the other nonsense taken place.

Long-Term Debt Maturities

This disclosure shows how much of long-term debt must be paid in each of the next five years and how much thereafter. This is useful in determining future cash flow and financing needs. Future lease payment obligations are also disclosed, but probably under a separate section.

Property and Casualty Insurance

Discloses whether the company has sufficient insurance to protect it against the types of risks it may face and whether its coverage meets normal and customary requirements for its industry.

Transactions with Insiders or Related Entities

Discloses the nature and terms of any business transactions with management or directors of the companies or entities that are owned or controlled by members of management or directors of the company. Also any transactions with companies in which the subject company has an ownership interest. Transactions might include sales to, purchases from, or loans to or from these parties or entities. These disclosures should be accompanied by a statement to the effect that the transactions were on terms no more or less favorable than those available through unrelated parties or entities. Otherwise these transactions could impair or distort financial results by making one company temporarily look more or less favorable at the expense of or to the benefit of another company or party.

Major Customers and/or Suppliers

Discloses whether there are any customers or suppliers which constitute such an unusually large portion of the company's business that the company may be highly vulnerable to a loss of such customers or suppliers. Gives the percent of sales to or purchases from these parties but not necessarily their names.

Industry Segment Information

Shows the amount of sales by product line and sometimes by geographic area. The latter is usually important when a lot of the sales are to foreign countries and may be affected by the volatility of exchange markets or their local political developments.

Current Cost or Replacement Value of Nonmonetary Assets

Discloses the current cost or replacement value of assets that are nonmonetary and are thus by their very nature not already stated at current cost values. Monetary assets include cash, accounts receivable, and marketable securities. Nonmonetary assets include inventory, property, plant, equipment, and intangibles. The latter are valued at historical cost on the financial statements, and therefore their current cost, or the cost of replacing them at current prices, is not reflected. Many companies find it useful to disclose current replacement costs in their footnotes.

Contingent Liabilities

Discloses current developments that may give rise to future obligations on the part of the company. The most prominent of these are usually pending lawsuits or regulatory actions. Where possible, an assessment of the future outcome and its impact on the company should be included. In practice, however, the company will always say that it doesn't have any idea what the outcome will be or that it expects to prevail and/or doesn't think that the whole thing amounts to a hill of beans. Were it to feel otherwise, it would have had to establish an estimated liability or reserve on its balance sheet with a corresponding charge against its current income.

Events Subsequent to the Date of the Financial Report

Discloses any material developments that occur after the rest of the report has been written, with presumably enough information so that the reader might form an opinion as to how they might affect the company's financial performance. For example, "The Company's factory blew up on March 3 . . ."

Many other kinds of disclosures may appear in the footnotes to companies' financial statements, but the preceding are among the most common.

A particularly memorable example of a disclosure that comes to mind was a high-tech medical device manufacturer's revelation that it didn't carry product liability insurance because such insurance would have been prohibitively expensive. Whatever the expense, it would be useful for a user of the statement to charge that amount against income in his own analysis to approximate the cost of not having the insurance. Risk tolerance or aversion was also an issue. (The company's bankers were not happy with the disclosure.)

OPINION LETTERS

The final item, which is an integral part of the financial statements, is the outside auditor's opinion letter. (When it is stated that something is "an integral part" of the financial statements, it means that you can't take the statements seriously without it.) The opinion letter for an audited statement should state that the audit has been performed in accordance with Generally Accepted Auditing Standards and that the statements were prepared in conformity with Generally Accepted Accounting Principles or that they fairly present the financial position, operating results, and cash flow of the company.

The opinion letter will also tell whether in fact the financial statements have been audited at all. Not all financial statements are audited. In fact, most are not. If you're not a banker or a credit manager, however, you're probably used to seeing only the financial statements of large, publicly owned companies. These have to be audited.

In addition to audited statements, there are *reviewed* statements and *compiled* statements, also known as *reviews* and *compilations*. Anything other than these three is not given any official status under GAAP and is therefore unfit for human consumption. Such maverick statements can conform to whatever rules or lack of rules the preparer wants them to and should only be used for internal company purposes or by hooligans who don't give a hoot about GAAP and all it stands for.

The difference between the three legitimate types of statements is in the level of assurance that each provides, or, in other words, how comfortable you ought to be with the notion that the company is what it purports to be. Examples of opinion letters for each of the three are shown in Exhibit 11–1.

Audited statements offer the highest level of assurance. They must be audited by independent accountants, so you

EXHIBIT 11–1

AUDIT

Report of Independent Public Accountants

To the Stockholders and Board of Directors of Diversified Consolidated Corp.

We have audited the accompanying consolidated balance sheets of Diversified Consolidated Corp. and subsidiaries as of December 31, 1992 and 1991, and the related consolidated statements of income, retained earnings, and cash flows for each of the three years in the period ended December 31, 1992. These financial statements are the responsibility of the Company's management. Our responsibility is to express an opinion on these financial statements based on our audits.

We conducted our audits in accordance with Generally Accepted Auditing Standards. Those standards require that we plan and perform the audit to obtain reasonable assurance about whether the financial statements are free of material misstatement. An audit includes examining, on a test basis, evidence supporting the amounts and disclosures in the financial statements. An audit also includes assessing the accounting principles used and significant estimates made by management, as well as evaluating the overall financial statement presentation. We believe that our audits provide a reasonable basis for our opinion.

In our opinion, the financial statements referred to above present fairly, in all material respects, the financial position of Diversified Consolidated Corp. and subsidiaries as of December 31, 1992 and 1991, and the results of their operations and their cash flows for each of the three years in the period ended December 31, 1992, in conformity with Generally Accepted Accounting Principles.

As discussed in the accompanying notes to financial statements, effective January 1, 1992, the Company adopted three new accounting standards promulgated by the Financial Accounting Standards Board, changing its methods of accounting for postretirement benefits other than pensions, income taxes, and postemployment benefits.

REVIEW

We have reviewed the accompanying balance sheet of Diversified Consolidated Corp., the related statement of earnings, and the related statement of changes in financial position for the year ended December 31, 1989, in accordance with standards established by the American Institute of Certified Public Accountants. All information included in these financial statements is the representation of the management of the Company.

A review consists principally of inquiries of company personnel and analytical procedures applied to financial data. It is substantially less in scope than an examination in accordance with Generally Accepted Auditing Standards, the objective of which is the expression of an opinion regarding the financial statements taken as a whole. Accordingly, we do not express such an opinion.

Based on our reviews, we are not aware of any material modifications that should be made to the accompanying financial statements in order for them to be in conformity with Generally Accepted Accounting Principles.

---

know, among other things, that the guys vouching for the numbers don't own a piece of the company.[1] While the accountants' ever-increasing and justifiable fear of lawsuits has caused them to emphasize of late that the financial statements are "the responsibility of management," at least at the audited level the accountants independently verify some of the things management tells them.

The accountants therefore confirm bank balances with the bank, accounts receivable balances with customers, and accounts payable balances with suppliers. They supervise

---

[1] The extent to which their income depends on this company (make that *customer*) may nevertheless be a matter of concern.

COMPLICATION

Board of Directors

The accompanying balance sheet of Diversified Consolidated Corp. as at December 31, 1989, and the related operating statement for the twelve-month period then ended have been compiled by me.

A compilation is limited to presenting in the form of financial statements information that is the representation of management. I have not audited or reviewed the accompanying financial statements and, accordingly, do not express an opinion or any form of assurance.

Management has elected to omit all of the disclosures and the Statement of Changes in Financial Position required by Generally Accepted Accounting Principles. If the omitted disclosures were included in the financial statements, they might influence the user's conclusion about the Company's financial position, results of operations, and changes in financial position. Accordingly, these financial statements are not designed for those who are not informed about such matters.

the annual inventory count. They also determine whether reasonable methodology was used in arriving at asset values, whether the company owns things it says it owns, and, in general, whether all accounts and statements have been prepared properly. They also test the adequacy of the company's own internal accounting and controls.

The opinion letter for the audited statement says something to the effect that, "We're pretty sure these statements are OK, and we've even done some independent checking to assure us that they are. But if management has done anything really sleazy to mislead us, don't hold us responsible for that."

Reviewed financial statements must also be reviewed by independent accountants but offer a lower level of assurance that everything is what it is supposed to be. More emphasis is placed on "the responsibility of management." (Translation: "Go sue *them*.") The accountants really don't have any well-defined responsibility to independently verify anything unless something jumps right out at them and screams for investigation.

Review-level statements basically mean that the accountants checked the procedures and presentation for conformity with GAAP and didn't see anything unusual in the numbers that would cause them to be suspicious.

That's very unfortunate and dangerous because it tells us that if everything appears to be normal no special effort will be given to verifying management's representations, when in fact it is the unusual occurrences disguised as normal that we ought to fear the most.

The review-level opinion letter says, in essence, that the accountants think that the financial statements are OK because management says so and nothing sticks out that would indicate otherwise. The accountants may provide additional testing of the numbers, but they don't have to.

A compilation statement offers the lowest level of assurance and does not need to be prepared by an independent accountant. However, if the accountant is not independent, he is required to disclose that he is not. Presumably it is up to the reader of the statement to find out exactly why the accountant cannot be considered independent.

Compilation statements may or may not contain the footnoted disclosures required by GAAP. If they do not, they must point out that they do not. At its worst, the compilation means that the statements are "the representation of management" and may well omit so much critical information as to be totally misleading to anyone who doesn't already know all about the company. That's pretty much what the opinion letter for the compilation statement without disclosures required by GAAP says.

Opinion letters may also be classified as to whether the opinions are qualified or unqualified. A *qualified* opinion is one that is given "subject to" some irregularity being resolved in such a way that it doesn't totally decimate the company, or at least cause it serious damage. Generally that means that the company's financial presentation contains a material departure from GAAP that may distort its performance or that there is a material risk that cannot be quantified but may severely affect the company's financial position or performance.

For companies that are really on thin ice, there is a *going concern* qualification that states that asset values reflect the value to the company as a going concern and may not accurately reflect liquidation value.

Needless to say, unqualified opinions are greatly preferred over qualified opinions.

In spite of the language in opinion letters and an occasional accounting scandal here or there, the overwhelming majority of accountants do an excellent job of assuring that the financial statements fairly represent the company's financial position and performance. The opinion letters are just worded cautiously so that we don't get too mad at the accountants if they do screw up.

Chapter Twelve

Some Basic Tools of Financial Analysis

So far, we have looked at financial statements as a compilation of isolated account balances. Sure, we know how to include inventory in the calculation of cost of goods sold and how to subtract these costs and other expenses from revenue to get net income. We also know what each account represents in the company's overall financial picture.

The user of financial statements, however, needs more than just a knowledge of the meaning of the principal components of the statements. He needs to be able to paint a picture of a company's successes and failures, its strengths and weaknesses, and whether its future appears to be bright or cloudy.

WHAT DO WE NEED TO KNOW?

In order to paint such a picture, we need to understand relationships between certain key items in the financial statements. We need to know how these relationships compare to other representative companies in the same industry and how these relationships are changing over time.

HOW FINANCIAL RATIOS CAN HELP

Relationships are analyzed by means of ratios that compare one account or group of accounts to another at a given point in time as well as over a period of time. Since most readers of this book probably do not intend to become financial analysts, it is not expected that you will regularly calculate these ratios every time you look at a financial statement. It is, however, important that you be aware of what ratios are critical and for what purpose.

Even if you do not perform the calculations, you should probably get in the habit of roughly comparing certain accounts to others to which they have a special relationship every time you look at a set of financial statements. In this way, you will acquire an awareness or sense of what appears to be reasonable and what appears to be out of line.

To really understand the changes taking place within a company, however, you should calculate key ratios and study their changes over time. This is not difficult to do. In this chapter, we discuss various ratios and what they can tell us about a company.

Let's start with a rather simple example of why ratios are important. As depicted in Exhibit 12–1, Company A has a net worth, or owners' equity, or $100.0 million, while Company B has a net worth of only $10.0 million. Which is the stronger company?

You don't know is absolutely the correct answer. Give yourself an A + , and consider the following additional information. Company A has total assets of $600.0 million, while Company B has assets of only $20.0 million. What's this? Something suspicious. Company A has 10 times the net worth of Company B but 30 times the amount of assets. Since the difference between assets and net worth is liabilities, Company A has $500.0 million in liabilities against its $600.0 million in assets, while Company B has only $10.0 million in liabilities against its assets of $20.0 million (see Exhibit 12–2).

Company A's ratio of total liabilities to net worth is 5.0 to 1.0, while Company B's is only 1.0 to 1.0. Why should we care? The ratio of total liabilities to net worth is a measure of a company's leverage. Leverage was discussed briefly in

EXHIBIT 12-1
Net Worth Comparison

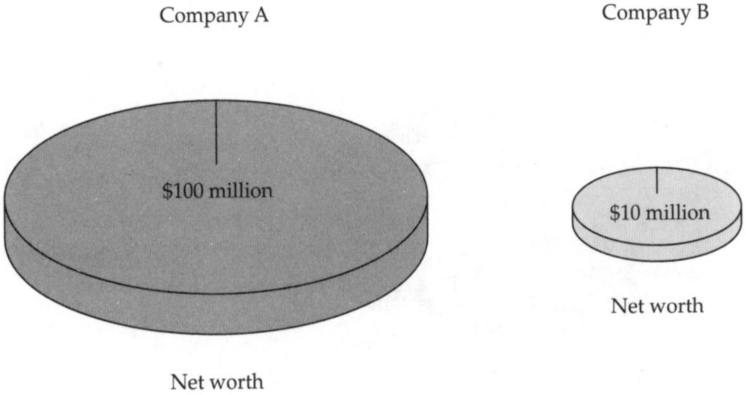

Company A   Company B

$100 million

$10 million

Net worth

Net worth

Chapter Four, where we observed that too much leverage limits a company's options in dealing with adversity.

As an example of how leverage can work against a company, let's assume that each of our subject companies goes through some very tough economic times and suffers a 20.0 percent decline in the value of its assets. For this illustration, the decline could have been caused by either operating losses that were funded by a reduction in assets or a direct write down to reflect a decline in the market value of existing assets. No matter. In either case, there is a reduction in net worth, caused by the operating losses or the asset revaluation, offset by a reduction in total assets.

The difference in the impact on the companies is that 20.0 percent of Company A's $600.0 million is $120.0 million, and Company A's entire net worth before the devaluation is only $100.0 million. For Company B, on the other hand, 20.0 percent of $20.0 million in total assets represents only $4.0 million compared to its net worth of $10.0 million.

While a 40.0 percent reduction in its net worth is certainly no laughing matter to Company B, Company A has lost all

EXHIBIT 12–2
Liabilities in Relation to Net Worth

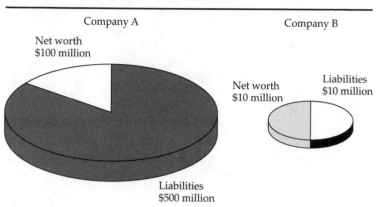

of its net worth and then some. It is, at least theoretically, wiped out.

Some analysts look at the ratio of debt to net worth instead of total liabilities to net worth. That calculation leaves things like accrued expenses and accounts payable out of the liability side of the ratio. This writer prefers to include all liabilities in the calculation, but, in any case, some measure of leverage is always in order when performing financial analysis.

Leverage ratios are by no means the only measure of a company's financial health or viability, but they are among the more important ones. Leverage ratios, moreover, need to be observed over a period of time. A company with high leverage may be so immensely profitable that its leverage, while high, is declining rapidly. Another may have lower leverage but is either suffering losses funded by additions to debt or funding growth in a profitable business with quantities of debt well out of proportion to the increases in net worth generated by its profits.

It should also be understood that leverage, while commonly and appropriately associated with risk, is not necessarily bad. For any company, there is an optimal level of leverage that enables it to maximize its profits without undue risk. Otherwise why would any company voluntarily take on any debt at all? (Some companies increase their liabilities *involuntarily* to fund operating losses.)

The whole premise behind the use of debt, or any other liabilities, is that the company can invest the funds owed in assets that will generate a higher rate of return (i.e., profits) than the cost of borrowing the funds. That's just sound business, as it can substantially increase the rate of return on owners' equity. It is therefore only the excessive use of debt that subjects the company to undue risk.

While being lightly leveraged may therefore be a safer course of action, it is not necessarily the most profitable one. Just as inordinate amounts of leverage were criticized in the 1980s and early 90s, the failure to use even reasonable levels of leverage to take advantage of profitable opportunities had been criticized in earlier periods.

The whole cycle of underutilization and overutilization of leverage can be expected to repeat itself in future years. Ecclesiastes was probably referring to business cycles when he said that there wasn't anything new under the sun.

SOME USEFUL RATIOS AND WHAT THEY TELL US

To decide what ratios to analyze, we must first decide what kind of financial information we need to know about a company. The following is a list of questions we might wish to resolve and the financial ratios best suited to provide the answers:

1. Is the value of the company's assets sufficient to cover claims of creditors against these assets and still provide adequate equity for the owners'?

Leverage ratio: Total liabilities divided by owners' equity.

2. Does the company have sufficient liquidity to pay its bills?
Quick or liquidity ratio: Total of cash, short-term marketable securities and accounts receivable divided by current liabilities (i.e., liabilities that need to be paid within one year).

Current ratio: Total current assets (convertible into cash within one year) divided by total current liabilities. The major difference between the current ratio and the quick ratio is that the former includes inventory in current assets on the assumption that it can be sold and the proceeds collected within one year.

3. Is the company's cash flow before debt payments sufficient to cover debt obligations by a reasonable margin?

Debt coverage ratio: This one is calculated in many different ways. Let's use the total of net income and noncash charges divided by current maturities of long-term debt. There are other options that analysts will argue give a better picture of debt payment capacity. They all argue vigorously for their own approach, so there may be some sour grapes because we didn't choose someone's favorite method. Ours is both useful and simple, and, in any case, the statement of cash flows gives a complete picture of all sources and uses of cash for those of you who want to play around with it.

4. Is the company able to collect its accounts receivable promptly? (If we're going to give the receivables credit for liquidity in the liquid ratio, they ought to be liquid.)

Accounts receivable collection period: Accounts receivable divided by sales for the period times the number of days in period. For example, a company has annual sales of $1.0 million and accounts receivable of $200,000. The collection period is: 200,000 ÷ 1,000,000 × 365 = 73 days.

5. *Is the company carrying the proper amount of inventory to support its level of sales?*

Days inventory supply: Inventory divided by cost of goods sold for the period times number of days in period. For example, the company with $1.0 million in sales has a cost of goods sold for the year of $700,000 and ending inventory of $150,000. Its inventory supply is therefore: 150,000 ÷ 700,000 × 365 = 78.2 days.

Too much inventory increases the likelihood that the inventory is not selling at the prices expected and will have to be liquidated at a loss. It is also a drain on the company's resources, as increasing inventory is a use of cash.

Too little inventory increases the likelihood that the company will not be able to meet the demand for its product and will lose customers or potential customers. Securities analysts worry about this problem more than bankers do, as bankers worry far more about downside risk than upside potential.

Theoretically, at the current rate of sales and cost of goods sold, the company's inventory would last 78.2 days if it stopped production immediately. That's fine (theoretically) for a distributor of completed products, but for a manufacturer it doesn't take into account the mix among raw materials, work in process, and finished goods. It can still be used as a rough estimate for comparative purposes as long as we understand its limitations.

The mix of inventory can be every bit as important as the amount. A company that has a lot of raw materials and work in process but very little finished product has probably stepped up production in response to strong demand for its product. A company with lots of finished product and very little raw materials or work in process may well be stuck with product it has completed but cannot sell. It may therefore have cut back on additional purchases and production.

6. *Are the company's assets producing sufficient income relative to alternative investment opportunities?*

Return on assets (ROA): Net income divided by total assets. This number, expressed as a percentage, should at least exceed that which is available through investment in minimal risk alternatives, such as short-term U.S. Treasury securities. Otherwise the company is not receiving an adequate return on its investment in its assets. If, for example, 90-day Treasury bills are yielding 5 percent and a company's ROA is only 3 percent on more than just a temporary basis, the company would be better off investing in Treasury bills than operating its business.

7. *Is the company generating sufficient income to be a worthwhile investment for its owners?*

Return on equity (ROE): Net income divided by owners' (shareholders') equity. This number, also expressed as a percentage, should be well in excess of the risk-free rate of return available on alternative investments to reward investors for taking the risk of investing for a profit that is not assured. In the example under question 6 above, this return should probably be in excess of 8 percent—hopefully well in excess. Like all other financial ratios, however, the ROE would be used to measure this company relative to its peers.

There are many other ratios that are widely inspected with varying degrees of usefulness. As we have seen, the gross profit margin (gross profit divided by sales) measures the contribution the company's product makes toward all other expenses and to net profits. The greater the gross profit margin, the more the company is able to spend in areas like marketing or research and development, which should increase its competitive advantages in future periods.

Various operating expense ratios, defined as operating expenses divided by sales, are also most useful. Once a company is beyond its start-up stage, operating expenses should not increase as fast as sales. In an efficient company, a given level of property and equipment and management expenses (including marketing, research and development, etc.) should generate increasing levels of sales for some time to come with only slight increases in these expenses relative to sales. Therefore, operating expense ratios should decline as sales increase.

If they consistently fail to do so, that means that the company is spending increasing amounts on operating expenses just to maintain a given level of sales. It is then useful to isolate those specific categories of expenditures that are rising faster than sales.

If, for example, research and development as a percent of sales is rising, that means that the company is having to spend increasing amounts on research and development just to stay even with its competition. If marketing is the culprit, the company is spending too much on its sales efforts in relation to the result they are producing. These trends are meaningful, however, only when analyzed over a period of years, as operating expenses and the revenues they generate may be erratic from one period to another.

The foregoing analytical tools should provide a good start without burying the reader in ratios. To get a feel for some actual financial ratios, refer to excerpts from *Robert Morris Associates Annual Statement Studies 1992* in the Appendix at the end of this book. RMA publishes a compilation of ratios for various industries with averages as well as 25- and 75-percentile levels for each ratio for each industry. We have reproduced the data for Manufacturers of Electronic Components and for Advertising Agencies as examples for a manufacturing and a service company.

There are also clear limitations to the effectiveness of these ratios under different scenarios, but the best way to understand them is to use them in an analysis of a sample company. We can assess their usefulness and their limitations in describing what is happening to The Easy Company in Chapter Thirteen.

Chapter Thirteen

Application of Financial Ratios to Analysis of the Growth of The Easy Company

Let's go back to The Easy Company, our manufacturer of user-friendly toothpicks through which we illustrated the fundamentals of financial statements in Chapters Four through Six. The Easy Company has been highly profitable and is in excellent financial condition as evidenced by the ratios for 1992 shown in the first column of Exhibit 13–1. The company has very little leverage and far more than adequate liquidity to meet its current obligations. Its income and noncash charges, moreover, cover its current maturities of long-term debt ($200,000 per year) by a margin of 4.0 to 1.0 (see Exhibit 13–2).

The only areas of weakness for The Easy Company are its accounts receivable collection period, which at 91 days is a bit slow, and its inventory supply, which at 120 days is somewhat excessive.

The Easy Company can afford to be a little lax, given its strong condition, and doesn't like to hassle its customers for quick payment on its receivables. It is generally regarded, in this and other respects, as being "easy" to do business with. It also likes to carry plenty of inventory so that it knows it can always be viewed as a dependable supplier.

EXHIBIT 13–1
The Easy Company Financial Highlights

	1992	1993	1994	1995	1996	1997
Sales	$10,000,000	$12,000,000	$15,000,000	$16,000,000	$14,000,000	$10,000,000
Cost of goods sold	7,000,000	8,400,000	11,100,000	12,000,000	10,500,000	8,000,000
Gross margin (%)	3,000,000 (30%)	3,600,000 (30%)	3,900,000 (26%)	4,000,000 (25%)	3,500,000 (25%)	2,000,000 (26%)
Operating expenses (%)	2,000,000 (20%)	3,000,000 (25%)	3,000,000 (20%)	3,200,000 (20%)	3,220,000 (23%)	3,000,000 (30%)
Income before taxes	1,000,000	600,000	900,000	800,000	280,000	(1,000,000)
Taxes (40%)	400,000	240,000	360,000	320,000	112,000	(400,000)
Net income	600,000	360,000	540,000	480,000	168,000	(600,000)
Depreciation	200,000	280,000	350,000	400,000	460,000	540,000
Cash flow for debt maturities	$ 800,000	$640,000	$890,000	$880,000	$628,000	$(60,000)
Cash	$ 900,000	$500,000	$500,000	$500,000	$500,000	$500,000
Marketable securities	1,000,000	1,000,000	1,000,000	500,000	500,000	500,000
Accounts receivable	2,500,000	3,452,000	5,137,000	6,575,300	6,520,500	4,794,500
Inventory	2,300,000	2,991,800	4,561,600	5,260,300	5,178,100	4,383,600
Prepaid expenses	100,000	100,000	100,000	100,000	100,000	100,000

Total current assets	6,800,000	8,043,800	11,298,600	12,935,600	12,798,600	10,278,100
Investment in affiliate	200,000	200,000	200,000	200,000	200,000	200,000
Property, plant, and equipment	2,800,000	3,500,000	4,000,000	4,600,000	5,400,000	5,400,000
Total assets	$10,000,000	$11,743,800	$15,498,600	$17,735,600	$18,398,600	$15,878,100
Current liabilities	$ 1,900,000	$3,283,800	$6,498,600	$8,255,600	$8,750,000	$6,830,100
Long-term debt	1,800,000	1,800,000	1,800,000	1,800,000	1,800,000	1,800,000
Total liabilities	3,700,000	5,083,800	8,298,600	10,055,600	10,550,000	8,630,100
Owners' equity	6,300,000	6,660,000	7,200,000	7,680,000	7,848,000	7,248,000
Total liability and equity	$10,000,000	$11,743,800	$15,498,600	$17,735,600	$18,398,600	$15,878,100
Leverage ratio	.6	.8	1.2	1.3	1.3	1.2
Liquid ratio	2.4	1.5	1.0	.9	.9	.8
Current ratio	3.6	2.4	1.7	1.6	1.5	1.5
Debt service coverage	4.0	3.2	4.5	4.4	3.1	NA
Account receivables collection period	91	105	125	150	170	175
Inventory supply	120	130	150	160	180	200

EXHIBIT 13–2
The Easy Company Financial Ratios

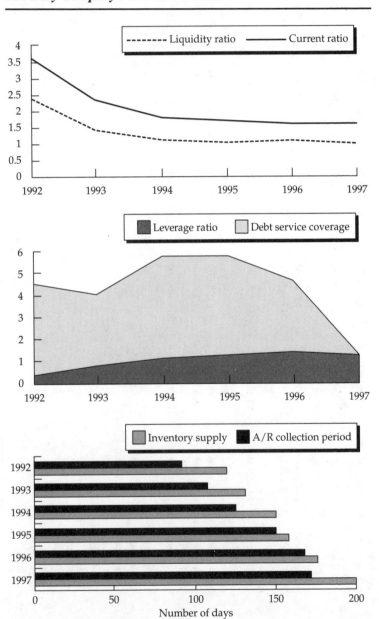

STRATEGY AND ANALYSIS

The Easy Company, however, is a bit uneasy about its lack of diversification. It therefore decides to come out with a new line of designer toothpicks, which it is convinced will sell like hotcakes. (The company had previously rejected a proposal to diversify into hotcakes as being too risky.)

Easy decides to facilitate the production and sale of its new line through massive investments in new plant and equipment to provide generous amounts of inventory and by assuring its customers it will continue not to hassle them for payment until they are convinced the new product is a winner. The results in Exhibit 13–1 reflect these policies.

Sales are in line with expectations for the first three years, although growth did weaken a bit in 1995. The fourth and fifth years, however, are clearly disappointing. Designer toothpicks ultimately prove to be a fad for happy-go-lucky yuppies, and an austere economic climate causes customers to cut back on their purchases of luxury goods like designer toothpicks.

Easy's gross margins, its gross profit as a percent of sales, declined over four of the five years as higher production costs of designer toothpicks exceeded any benefit the company could achieve through premium pricing. Prices were cut sharply in 1997 as an effort to stimulate lagging sales. Operating expenses increased in 1993 as the company geared up for its new product launch. The company was not very successful in cutting these expenses when sales declined.

The Easy Company slowly and reluctantly cut back on production when sales began to decline, as they didn't "want to look like a bunch of losers." While inventory eventually declined, inventory supply increased, as sales (at cost) showed a larger percentage decline than inventory.

Customers, who were skeptical of the product from the beginning and were therefore slow to pay the receivables, became irritated at being "hassled for payment" when their own sales turned weak. The receivables collection period therefore grew longer.

Easy had funded the entire expansion program with bank loans and increases in accounts payable for its inventory purchases. Its bank had tried to get the company to finance its plant and equipment with longer-term debt to match the useful lives of the assets, but Easy felt it had the resources to pay off the debt quickly. Easy also decided to maintain at least $500,000 in cash plus an additional $500,000 in marketable securities at all times as a safety net.

While net income plus noncash charges did not turn negative until 1997, uses of cash for accounts receivable, inventory, and equipment exceeded sources before financing in each of the first three years. Liquidity therefore declined steadily over the period, but the rate of decline slowed a bit as the company's growth slowed and then reversed.

Leverage increased sharply in the first two years, peaked during the next two, and declined slightly in 1997 when sources of cash from asset reductions slightly exceeded cash used to pay down liabilities and cover net losses.

Due to its strong financial position and profitability at the outset, Easy's miscalculations have thus far not proven disastrous to the company. Its financial position has deteriorated significantly, but from very strong to not too bad. Its receivables collection period and inventory supply, however, are now far too high.

PROFITABILITY AND ASSET MANAGEMENT

Whether Easy can prevent further deterioration that could cause it more serious problems depends on the reversal of a combination of adverse trends. It needs to restore profitability by getting its gross profit margins back to earlier levels and reducing its operating expenses. To restore its gross margins, it needs to either increase prices or cut costs. Its best bet may be to return to its former product mix, which apparently yielded a very profitable level of sales at pricing that allowed for good profit margins.

In addition, Easy needs to manage its assets better. The company's carefree attitudes toward accounts receivable collection and inventory supply have hurt both its cash flow and its financial position. Increases in accounts receivable and inventory are uses of cash and, if not offset by other asset reductions or increases in owners' equity (sources of cash), require that cash be provided by increasing liabilities or a reduction in actual cash balances (additional sources of cash).

To be sure, there are points at which tight receivables collection policies and limited inventory supplies can cause a loss of customers, which would have a detrimental effect on the performance and financial position of the firm. The trick is to find the optimal levels or policies for each asset so as to maximize sales and profits without causing undue risk and financial strain on the company.

For analytical purposes, there are two components of increases or decreases in accounts receivable and inventory, each of which says something different about management. One is the amount of change caused by a change in the level of sales and cost of goods sold. That can be calculated by applying the former collection period or inventory days supply to the new level of sales or cost of goods sold. The second is caused by management policies and effectiveness. This can be measured by the difference between the calculated change based on a constant collection period or inventory supply and the actual change. As an example, we can look at these calculations for The Easy Company between 1992 and 1995:

	1992	*1995*
Revenue	$10,000,000	$16,000,000
AR collection period	91 days	150 days
1995 AR at 1992 collection period		
(16MM × 91 ÷ 365)		$3,989,000
Actual 1995 AR		$6,575,300
Increase due to management		$2,586,300
Cost of goods sold	$7,000,000	$12,000,000
Inventory supply	120 days	160 days
1995 inventory at 1992 days supply		
(12MM × 120 ÷ 365)		$3,945,200
Actual 1995 inventory		$5,260,300
Increase due to management		$1,315,100

In summary, we may observe that growth is generally healthy for a company, but an excessive rate of growth can be hazardous. Whether a company can maintain its level of growth without impairing its financial position depends on the degree to which it can generate sources of funds or control uses of funds so that its financing needs do not become excessive. The healthiest source of funds for a growing company is profits. Other things being equal, companies with high profit margins can sustain a higher level of growth than those with lower margins.

Asset management, as we have seen, is a critical element in the constraint of cash outflows, or uses of cash. To the extent that a company's rate of asset expansion is no greater than (or even less than) its rate of sales growth, it can sustain that level of growth without incurring an excessive financing burden to fund its asset growth.

In fact, companies can also improve their cash flow and financial position while suffering declining sales and even operating losses by efficient asset management. Reductions in assets can produce more cash and/or debt reduction than losses consume, resulting in liabilities declining at a greater rate than equity. This is strictly a short-term phenomenon, however, as asset reduction in the face of losses should never be viewed as a recurring source of cash flow.

DEFENSIVE VERSUS OPPORTUNISTIC DIVERSIFICATION

Finally, a word about diversification. Many companies speak of diversification as a way of lessening the impact of setbacks in existing businesses or as the quickest path to growth. One might well imagine that it is easier to grow faster by being in five or six markets than by being in only one.

One can observe, however, two different motivations for diversification that are not mutually exclusive but often receive far different emphasis. One we will call *defensive* diversification, the other *opportunistic* diversification.

The first arises more from serious problems that a company is facing or is about to face in its existing markets. The company may no longer be able to grow or even maintain its existing market share. Whatever the reason, the company sees diversification as a necessity. It may therefore be less discriminating in its selection of an acquisition or in its development of a new service or product line. It has to make this move, so the only requirement is to make the best selection available to it at the time.

A company that is strong and growing in its current product or service lines has no reason for diversification other than that an opportunity with unusual profit potential has presented itself. While the company may see some prudent diversification as healthy in the long run, it is certainly under no pressure to make any acquisition that does not meet its criteria for profitability and risk aversion.

It is important to determine a company's underlying motivation for diversification as well as the apparent benefits of the acquisition or expansion itself. Too many companies that have diversified as a largely defensive measure have served only to compound their problems.

None of this is to say that a company that needs to expand for defensive reasons cannot hit upon a good opportunity or that a strictly opportunistic company cannot make a bad acquisition. It is just to say that it is less likely than the other way around.

Chapter Fourteen

The Limitations of Financial Statements

Many lenders and investors like to say that financial statements aren't important—that it's *management* that counts. These lenders and investors are missing the point.

What are financial statements if not a record of the strengths and weaknesses of management? True, a new management team might demonstrate different results than prior management, so one would presumably evaluate the results of other companies managed by the new team for an assessment of its capabilities.

Often, however, highly regarded new management is unable to overcome the constraints of a company that has severe financial problems and is in a difficult competitive environment. So consider also the economic climate, industry trends, and the position of previous companies at which management established its record compared to the current situation it is attempting to manage.

Financial statements, moreover, must be judged as strictly historical measures of performance and as a fair representation of current condition. Their most serious limitation is that, in reality, practically everything in them, excepting cash and most liabilities, is based on forecasts, estimates, and assumptions. Some of these are just more reliable than others.

We have discussed estimates in the form of useful lives for equipment and forecasts of motion picture and insurance premium revenues. The limitations in these cases are clear. In the case of inventory, there are three or four ways to value it, so why would you believe any of them? In fact, we know that LIFO carries inventory at a cost of purchases that may have occurred many years ago.

In fact, one of the major problems with financial statements is that nonmonetary assets are carried at their historical costs, adjusted for depreciation and special write downs to reflect clear and material losses of economic value. Actual losses in economic value more likely occur in increments over a period of time before the company and its outside accountant lump them together and decide that they had better recognize them.

More important, however, statements of assets at historical cost may well result in a substantial understatement of asset values since the replacement cost or current market value may be well in excess of historical cost adjusted for depreciation. This is especially likely when depreciation is calculated on an accelerated basis. The current economic value of assets should be of far more interest to users of financial statements than historical cost-based figures because it more truly reflects what the company is worth.

Even sales and accounts receivable are recorded on the presumption that there will be no unusual returns of merchandise because it is damaged or defective or sometimes just because the buyer has changed his mind. Accounts receivable balances assume that an adequate provision has been made for bad debts. The amount of this provision is clearly an informed estimate.

Banks offer a special example of the uses and limitations of estimates in financial reporting. They are required to estimate future losses on loans currently outstanding and thereby establish a "loan loss reserve." Do they have any idea what these losses might be? Of course not. That's why banks always take special charges against income to beef up their loan loss reserves any time they are faced with an economic environment considerably worse than that which has immediately preceded it.

A final concern regarding asset values is that they presume that the company is a *going concern*. (Remember the outside auditors will qualify the statements if they feel this assumption is questionable.) That means that asset values are to be realized from expected future income that, in fact, may or may not ever be generated.

Furthermore, if a company does meet with sudden misfortune and a lender or investor expects to look to reported asset values as a means of recovering a loan or investment, that lender or investor will usually find that these assets are not worth anywhere near their reported value when the company really needs to sell all of them quickly. If the company's inventory were really worth what it said it was worth, it would be selling at its cost plus some amount of profit. If the company's plant and equipment were worth what it was said to be worth, it would be producing things that could be manufactured and sold profitably. If these kinds of things were happening, the company would be a healthy going concern and we wouldn't be worried about how much we could get by terminating its operations and selling off all of its assets.

The truth is that these asset values can be thrown out the window in a liquidation, which is when many users of financial statements need them the most. Often companies get into trouble precisely because the assets they have invested in no longer meet the needs of their markets. Even accounts receivable become far more difficult to collect when the customer doesn't expect to get any more product from this supplier.

Most of these limitations are somewhat mitigated by the fact that companies and their auditors continually review estimates and assumptions and make appropriate revisions as needed. Through such diligence, adjustments hopefully can be held to modest proportions in all but the most extreme scenarios.

Financial statements are therefore highly useful instruments of analysis in spite of their limitations, as long as these limitations are understood. Financial reporting is not an exact science, but it gives its users the clearest practical picture of what a company has accomplished and where it stands as of the reporting date. That beats following hunches and exhilarating press releases as a guide to informed decision making.

Appendix

Services—Advertising Agencies SIC# 7311

	Comparative Historical Data			Current Data Sorted by Sales					
---	6/30/89-3/31/90 ALL	4/1/90-3/31/91 ALL	4/1/91-3/31/92 ALL	0-1MM	148(4/1-9/30/91) 1-3MM	3-5MM	5-10MM	220(10/1/91-3/31/92) 10-25MM	25MM & OVER
Type of Statement									
Unqualified	30	28	34	1	1	5	7	9	11
Reviewed	119	113	102	5	37	21	24	11	4
Compiled	140	127	131	33	67	15	9	6	1
Tax Returns		4	7	4	2			1	
Other	74	95	94	18	34	15	14	5	8
Number of statements	363	367	368	61	141	56	54	32	24
	%	%	%	%	%	%	%	%	%
Assets									
Cash and equivalents	11.5	12.4	10.5	11.2	11.4	6.9	10.0	12.5	9.8
Trade receivables (net)	52.2	51.7	53.0	43.3	54.6	53.8	57.6	58.2	49.0
Inventory	4.4	4.4	4.1	5.2	3.7	4.1	4.2	2.3	5.9
All other current	3.4	3.8	3.7	3.0	3.6	4.3	3.6	4.4	3.4
Total current	71.6	72.3	71.2	62.8	73.3	69.0	75.5	77.4	68.1
Fixed assets (net)	18.4	17.9	17.5	23.4	17.3	19.7	13.7	10.4	16.4
Intangibles (net)	1.7	2.1	2.7	3.2	1.7	2.6	2.3	4.4	5.7
All other noncurrent	8.3	7.7	8.6	10.6	7.7	8.6	8.5	7.8	9.9
Total	100.0	100.0	100.0	100.0	100.0	100.0	100.0	100.0	100.0
Liabilities									
Notes payable—short-term	9.2	8.9	9.0	11.8	10.6	8.2	8.6	3.4	3.3
Cur. mat-L/T/D	3.3	3.4	3.4	6.9	2.8	3.6	2.2	2.1	2.0
Trade payables	35.9	35.5	36.1	24.6	34.9	35.5	44.6	45.4	42.8
Income taxes payable	.9	.7	.7	.5	1.1	.7	.3	.2	.5
All other current	12.3	13.1	12.8	10.9	10.9	13.5	15.3	17.6	14.7
Total current	61.5	61.5	62.0	54.7	60.2	61.5	71.0	68.7	63.3
Long-term debt	10.4	10.5	9.0	14.8	8.3	7.5	5.7	8.4	10.1
Deferred taxes	.9	.5	1.1	.1	1.2	2.0	.9	.7	1.2

	1.8		2.5		2.9	All other noncurrent		.7		2.4		3.2		6.2		2.4		4.7
	25.3		25.0		25.0	Net worth		29.7		27.9		25.8		16.1		19.8		20.6
	100.0		100.0		100.0	Total liabilities and net worth		100.0		100.0		100.0		100.0		100.0		100.0
						Income Data												
	100.0		100.0		100.0	Net sales		100.0		100.0		100.0		100.0		100.0		100.0
						Gross profit												
	97.4		97.4		97.6	Operating expenses		97.7		97.4		97.7		98.6		97.1		95.9
	2.6		2.6		2.4	Operating profit		2.3		2.6		2.3		1.4		2.9		4.1
	.3		.8		.5	All other expenses (net)		.5		.2		.9		.5		.3		1.6
	2.3		1.8		1.9	Profit before taxes		1.9		2.3		1.4		.9		2.6		2.5
						Ratios												
	1.6		1.6		1.5			2.3		1.6		1.5		1.3		1.4		1.3
	1.2		1.2		1.2	Current		1.3		1.2		1.1		1.1		1.1		1.1
	.9		1.0		.9			.8		1.0		.9		.9		1.0		.9
	1.3		1.4		1.4			1.6		1.4		1.4		1.2		1.2		1.1
	1.0		1.1		1.0	Quick		1.1		1.1		1.0		1.0		1.0		.9
	.8		.8		.8			.8		.9		.8		.8		.9		.7
37	10.0	38	9.7	38	9.6		23	15.7	35	10.3	40	9.2	40	9.2	41	8.9	41	8.9
54	6.8	54	6.8	53	6.9	Sales/Receivables	42	8.6	54	6.7	60	6.1	49	7.4	58	6.3	74	4.9
79	4.6	72	5.1	83	4.4		63	5.8	83	4.4	89	4.1	72	5.1	81	4.5	192	1.9
						Cost of sales/Inventory												
						Cost of sales/Payables												
	11.5		12.1		12.5			8.3		11.6		11.6		24.3		11.0		10.4
	33.4		37.7		40.0	Sales/Working capital		31.5		35.2		42.3		57.2		55.6		114.3
	−84.7		−137.4		−60.4			−29.8		−557.8		−36.2		−62.4		−101.3		−23.9

Appendix (continued)

Type of Statement	Comparative Historical Data			Current Data Sorted by Sales					
EBIT/Interest	(310) 8.3 / 3.0 / .6	(322) 10.3 / 3.6 / 1.0	(320) 10.2 / 3.9 / 1.0	(50) 6.1 / 1.4 / -2.0	(127) 12.0 / 4.1 / .5	(44) 7.1 / 2.6 / .6	(50) 6.6 / 2.8 / 1.4	(28) 19.0 / 4.4 / 1.8	(21) 5.6 / 2.7 / 1.3
Net profit + depr., dep., amort./Cur. mat. L/T/D	(162) 4.3 / 1.9 / .4	(159) 6.1 / 2.6 / 1.2	(150) 5.8 / 2.6 / .5	(18) 1.9 / .6 / -.6	(49) 5.1 / 1.7 / .3	(25) 6.6 / 1.9 / .5	(29) 4.7 / 2.4 / .9	(15) 5.1 / 2.0 / 1.0	(14) 3.9 / 2.5 / 1.8
Fixed/Worth	.3 / .6 / 2.6	.3 / .6 / 1.9	.3 / .6 / 1.9	.3 / .9 / 7.4	.3 / .6 / 1.8	.2 / .9 / 6.8	.4 / .6 / 2.5	.2 / .4 / 1.8	.4 / 1.3 / -19.1
Debt/Worth	1.5 / 3.4 / 16.1	1.5 / 3.6 / 8.1	1.4 / 3.8 / 11.5	.7 / 2.3 / 15.3	1.4 / 3.1 / 8.4	1.3 / 2.9 / 31.1	2.6 / 5.2 / 23.1	2.3 / 4.8 / 17.4	2.5 / 5.2 / -96.1
% profit before taxes/Tangible net worth	(311) 56.9 / 21.8 / 1.6	(316) 50.9 / 21.3 / 4.4	(311) 49.0 / 20.6 / 3.2	(49) 60.1 / 6.1 / -27.5	(127) 59.7 / 31.4 / .7	(45) 50.4 / 12.2 / 1.4	(46) 53.3 / 22.2 / 4.6	(27) 42.4 / 19.3 / 10.7	(17) 58.9 / 19.8 / 9.4

% profit before taxes/Total assets	13.9	11.6	12.7	18.4	17.2	8.8	7.6	10.8	6.9
	4.8	5.0	4.2	1.3	7.1	2.8	3.1	3.3	3.7
	.3	.1	-.9	-14.1	-.9	-.7	.3	1.8	.2
Sales/Net fixed assets	61.0	61.7	54.4	42.5	56.4	52.3	57.3	106.7	34.5
	27.3	28.0	25.7	18.6	28.6	20.6	28.1	43.4	11.2
	12.2	13.5	13.2	8.4	15.0	11.8	18.4	16.2	7.4
Sales/Total assets	4.8	4.9	5.1	5.2	5.4	5.2	4.7	5.1	5.1
	3.5	3.7	3.6	3.7	3.6	3.6	3.7	3.7	1.5
	2.4	2.4	2.1	2.1	2.3	1.8	2.6	2.0	.9
% depr., dep., amort./Sales (47)	.7	.6 (322)	.7	1.1 (125)	.7 (49)	.8 (50)	.5 (29)	.4 (22)	.9
(315) (321)	1.3	1.3	1.2	2.1	1.3	1.1	.9	.8	1.9
	2.8	2.3	2.4	3.1	2.1	2.6	1.4	1.8	3.5
% officers', directors', owners' comp/Sales (33)	4.8	4.6 (162)	4.3	6.2 (75)	4.9 (23)	4.4 (15)	3.5 (11)	2.1	
(162) (156)	7.2	7.4	6.9	13.2	7.0	6.5	5.3	2.9	
	10.7	11.7	12.8	23.5	11.3	9.8	6.9	15.2	
Net sales ($)	3061506M	2747012M	3023959M	36586M	252809M	216427M	363886M	548630M	1605821M
Total assets ($)	1039975M	1175695M	1693002M	14169M	90281M	113494M	127860M	263085M	1084113M

M = $ thousand   MM = $ million

Source: Reprinted with permission, copyright Robert Morris Associates 1992.

Manufacturers—Electronic Components and Accessories SIC# 3671 (72,74-79)

	Comparative Historical Data			Current Data Sorted by Sales					
Type of Statement					216(4/1-9/30/91)			309(10/1/91-3/31/92)	
				0-1MM	1-3MM	3-5MM	5-10MM	10-25MM	25MM & OVER
Unqualified	195	180	227	3	15	19	47	55	88
Reviewed	93	93	100	9	26	24	28	12	1
Compiled	96	87	80	14	33	21	9	3	
Tax returns		5	3		2			1	
Other	105	110	115	8	25	15	18	28	21
	6/30/89-3/31/90 ALL	4/1/90-3/31/91 ALL	4/1/91-3/31/92 ALL						
Number of statements	489	475	525	34	101	79	102	99	110
Assets	%	%	%	%	%	%	%	%	%
Cash and equivalents	8.1	8.6	9.3	10.9	8.9	7.8	6.6	8.4	13.4
Trade receivables-(net)	29.2	29.4	28.0	31.1	30.1	31.2	29.4	26.1	23.3
Inventory	28.9	27.8	28.1	23.8	30.4	29.5	30.0	28.6	24.0
All other current	2.3	2.5	2.2	1.4	1.8	1.8	1.4	2.0	4.0
Total current	68.5	68.2	67.6	67.1	71.2	70.3	67.5	65.1	64.7
Fixed assets (net)	25.1	24.7	25.0	23.5	23.4	22.6	24.1	27.6	27.0
Intangibles (net)	1.9	1.9	2.1	1.6	1.4	1.2	2.6	2.2	2.8
All other noncurrent	4.5	5.2	5.4	7.7	4.0	6.0	5.8	5.1	5.6
Total	100.0	100.0	100.0	100.0	100.0	100.0	100.0	100.0	100.0
Liabilities									
Notes payable—short-term	10.6	9.8	9.4	10.6	12.5	12.8	9.5	7.8	5.2
Cur. mat-L/T/D	4.2	4.3	4.3	3.9	5.4	4.3	4.9	4.5	2.8
Trade payables	14.1	14.9	14.7	14.1	16.0	18.1	14.6	13.3	12.4
Income taxes payable	1.0	1.1	.7	.4	.6	.6	.9	.6	.9
All other current	8.8	9.0	9.2	6.1	8.3	10.6	9.3	9.1	10.0
Total current	38.7	39.0	38.3	35.1	42.8	46.5	39.2	35.2	31.4
Long-term debt	15.1	15.4	15.0	21.0	14.6	14.0	11.7	17.5	15.1
Deferred taxes	.9	.9	.6	.3	.3	.4	.6	.6	1.0

	All other noncurrent / Net worth / Total liabilities and net worth	Income Data: Net sales / Gross profit / Operating expenses / Operating profit / All other expenses (net) / Profit before taxes	Ratios — Current	Quick	Sales/Receivables	Cost of sales/Inventory	Cost of sales/Payables	Sales/Working capital
Col 1	3.2 / 49.4 / 100.0	100.0 / 31.3 / 24.7 / 6.7 / 1.5 / 5.2	3.2 / 2.1 / 1.4	1.9 / 1.1 / .8	45 8.1 / 54 6.7 / 65 5.6	51 7.2 / 81 4.5 / 130 2.8	24 15.3 / 36 10.2 / 48 7.6	2.9 / 4.1 / 9.2
Col 2	2.3 / 44.3 / 100.0	100.0 / 28.8 / 23.5 / 5.3 / 1.5 / 3.8	3.0 / 1.8 / 1.4	1.6 / 1.0 / .7	40 9.1 / 49 7.5 / 60 6.1	48 7.6 / 74 4.9 / 118 3.1	19 18.9 / 32 11.4 / 41 8.8	3.7 / 6.3 / 15.1
Col 3	3.4 / 45.2 / 100.0	100.0 / 30.9 / 25.5 / 5.4 / 1.4 / 4.0	2.6 / 1.8 / 1.2	1.5 / .9 / .6	38 9.6 / 49 7.4 / 60 5.9	48 9.4 / 74 5.2 / 118 3.2	19 17.2 / 32 11.8 / 41 7.5	5.1 / 8.3 / 18.7
Col 4	1.6 / 37.5 / 100.0	100.0 / 32.3 / 28.9 / 3.4 / 1.4 / 2.0	2.3 / 1.4 / 1.1	1.3 / .8 / .6	37 9.8 / 47 7.7 / 59 6.2	42 8.6 / 72 5.1 / 114 3.2	21 17.3 / 41 9.0 / 60 6.1	5.2 / 9.9 / 30.7
Col 5	2.8 / 39.4 / 100.0	100.0 / 37.5 / 33.2 / 4.2 / 1.7 / 2.5	2.5 / 1.8 / 1.3	1.6 / .9 / .6	37 9.9 / 45 8.2 / 63 5.8	46 8.0 / 78 4.7 / 126 2.9	20 18.3 / 35 10.3 / 58 6.3	4.7 / 8.5 / 17.3
Col 6	8.9 / 34.6 / 100.0	100.0 / 40.7 / 37.6 / 3.1 / 1.0 / 2.1	3.6 / 2.2 / 1.3	2.4 / 1.3 / .6	33 11.2 / 42 8.7 / 68 5.4	23 15.8 / 66 5.5 / 122 3.0	11 34.4 / 24 15.5 / 87 4.2	4.0 / 8.3 / 25.3
Col 7	3.1 / 43.0 / 100.0	100.0 / 32.7 / 27.7 / 5.0 / 1.5 / 3.5	2.8 / 1.8 / 1.3	1.6 / 1.0 / .6	39 9.4 / 49 7.5 / 62 5.9	43 8.5 / 76 4.8 / 122 3.0	20 18.0 / 34 10.8 / 51 7.2	3.9 / 7.4 / 16.7
Col 8	2.9 / 41.8 / 100.0	100.0 / 33.3 / 28.3 / 5.0 / 1.7 / 3.3	2.9 / 1.9 / 1.2	1.6 / 1.0 / .6	41 9.0 / 51 7.2 / 66 5.5	41 8.8 / 74 4.9 / 122 3.0	20 18.4 / 34 11.2 / 54 6.8	3.9 / 7.2 / 18.9
Col 9	2.8 / 42.6 / 100.0	100.0 / 33.4 / 27.8 / 5.6 / 1.6 / 4.1	2.8 / 1.8 / 1.3	1.5 / 1.0 / .6	41 8.9 / 52 7.0 / 63 5.8	41 8.8 / 79 4.6 / 126 2.9	21 17.7 / 33 10.9 / 51 7.2	3.9 / 6.9 / 15.9

Appendix (concluded)

Type of Statement	Comparative Historical Data			Current Data Sorted by Sales					
EBIT/Interest	8.6 3.2 1.2 (443)	6.5 2.8 1.1 (427)	6.4 3.1 1.1 (479)	3.9 1.9 -.9 (27)	6.1 2.2 .6 (90)	5.1 1.7 1.0 (70)	6.4 3.0 1.4 (95)	6.6 3.3 1.5 (93)	9.0 4.1 1.3 (104)
Net profit + Depr., dep., amort./Cur. mat. L/T/D	6.6 2.7 1.1 (264)	4.9 2.1 1.0 (252)	5.8 2.4 .9 (276)	(48)	4.0 1.7 .5 (42)	3.4 1.9 1.0 (56)	7.2 2.3 1.2 (49)	3.6 1.9 .8 (75)	12.0 4.4 1.4
Fixed/Worth	.3 .6 1.3	.3 .6 1.3	.3 .6 1.2	.1 .7 2.8	.2 .5 1.3	.2 .6 1.5	.3 .5 1.3	.4 .7 1.1	.3 .6 1.1
Debt/Worth	.7 1.4 3.0	.6 1.4 3.4	.6 1.4 2.9	.7 2.3 8.0	.7 1.3 3.6	.8 1.9 3.7	.6 1.4 2.9	.7 1.4 2.6	.4 1.0 2.3
% profit before taxes/Tangible net worth	39.8 19.3 3.9 (463)	(439)	35.7 16.5 2.1 (493)	81.3 17.0 -4.5 (28)	38.9 12.3 -.3 (89)	39.1 11.9 1.6 (74)	32.6 16.0 5.0 (100)	37.9 17.9 6.7 (95)	32.0 17.4 3.3 (107)

	g1	g2	g3	g4	g5	g6	g7	g8	g9
% profit before taxes/Total assets	16.1 / 7.4 / 1.5	14.5 / 7.2 / 2.6	13.0 / 5.8 / 1.8	10.1 / 2.9 / .4	14.2 / 5.5 / -1.6	21.7 / 5.0 / -6.8	14.4 / 6.2 / .6	14.9 / 6.1 / .4	17.1 / 7.5 / .8
Sales/Net fixed assets	10.3 / 6.0 / 3.4	14.1 / 7.3 / 4.2	20.7 / 9.1 / 5.2	24.3 / 13.5 / 6.6	25.7 / 12.5 / 6.9	60.8 / 9.5 / 6.3	18.3 / 8.5 / 4.8	19.4 / 8.9 / 4.7	18.6 / 8.6 / 5.0
Sales/Total assets	2.0 / 1.4 / 1.1	2.6 / 1.9 / 1.3	2.6 / 2.1 / 1.6	2.8 / 2.2 / 1.7	2.8 / 2.2 / 1.7	3.3 / 2.0 / 1.5	2.6 / 2.0 / 1.4	2.6 / 1.9 / 1.4	2.6 / 2.0 / 1.5
% depr., dep., amort./Sales	(91) 2.2 / 3.5 / 5.4	(87) 1.6 / 2.6 / 4.5	(95) 1.2 / 2.5 / 4.0	(70) 1.2 / 2.4 / 4.0	(92) 1.4 / 2.1 / 3.9	(29) .7 / 2.2 / 6.9	(464) 1.5 / 2.6 / 4.4	(410) 1.4 / 2.7 / 4.6	(421) 1.6 / 2.8 / 4.8
% Officers', directors', owners' comp/Sales		(14) 1.6 / 2.1 / 3.4	(34) 1.9 / 3.4 / 7.0	(30) 3.0 / 5.6 / 9.5	(50) 4.2 / 6.9 / 11.3	(13) 7.2 / 12.3 / 23.3	(143) 2.8 / 5.3 / 9.7	(135) 3.0 / 5.1 / 10.6	(131) 2.4 / 5.3 / 9.0
Net sales ($)	10319209M	149351M	740498M	310609M	204885M	20387M	13090939M	9480200M	10006586M
Total assets ($)	7539973M	946821M	404949M	155624M	108330M	14474M	9170171M	6674078M	6870779M

M = $ thousand   MM = $ million

Source: Reprinted with permission, copyright Robert Morris Associates 1992.

Glossary of Terms

accelerated cost recovery system (ACRS) Internal Revenue Service guidelines for accelerated depreciation for tax reporting purposes.

accelerated depreciation Method that charges greater amounts of depreciation in earlier years of assets' life and lesser amounts in later years.

accounting The process of recording all of a company's financial transactions and developing and compiling the numbers to be used in a company's financial reports.

accounting period The period of time covered by a company's income statement, also the period of time between balance sheets.

accounts payable Money due to suppliers for products purchased or services received.

accounts receivable Money due from customers for products sold or services provided.

accounts receivable collection period Average number of days it takes to collect a company's accounts receivable.

accrual Income that has been earned but has not yet been received or expense that has been incurred but has not yet been paid. Also, process by which these items are recorded in financial reports.

accumulated depreciation Total of all periodic depreciation that has been charged against an asset or group of assets. Shown as a reduction to the asset's cost.

allowance for doubtful accounts Reduction in gross accounts receivable to allow for amounts that will not be collectible.

amortization Accounting process by which costs of intangible assets are charged to the periods over which they are expected to generate income.

asset That which is owned by a company and is expected to be used to generate future income.

audited financial statements Financial statements that offer the highest level of assurance by outside independent accountants that they constitute a fair presentation of company's financial position and operating results. Management representations are independently verified wherever possible.

average cost Method of inventory valuation that assumes inventory sold during period was purchased at the average cost of all inventory available for sale.

Balance Sheet Financial report that shows a company's assets, liabilities, and owners' equity as of a given date.

bond A marketable security representing long-term debt.

book value The value of an asset on a company's books or balance sheet, which is its historical cost adjusted for depreciation or amortization and any special write downs.

cash basis Recording income and expense at the time of cash receipt or payment.

cash equivalents Assets that will be converted to cash in a very short period of time (three months or less) with no market risk of loss in value.

cash flow The net amount of cash generated by a company in an accounting period.

compilation financial statement Type of financial statement offering the lowest level of assurance as to whether it is a fair presentation of a company's financial position and operations. Relies almost entirely on the representations of management.

conservatism Accounting principle that dictates use of the accounting method that presents results in the least favorable light whenever there is a choice between two otherwise acceptable methods.

consolidation Accounting for an ownership interest in another company by combining its financial statement accounts with that of the company that has the ownership interest.

contingent liability Something that will become a liability if and when a certain likely event or set of events occur. A dollar amount cannot be placed on the potential liability because of the uncertainty of the outcome.

contributed capital That part of owners' equity that has been contributed by investors as opposed to retained from income earned.

cost of goods sold The cost of any inventory sold during an accounting period on the books of the selling company.

current assets Assets that are expected to be converted to cash within one year through the company's normal operations.

current liabilities Liabilities that are due for payment within one year.

current maturities of long-term debt Payments due within one year on debt that was originally due over a longer period of time.

current ratio The ratio of current assets to current liabilities.

debt coverage ratio The ratio of a company's cash flow before investing and financing activities to its short-term debt maturities.

deferred taxes Taxes that have been recorded as an expense for financial reporting purposes but that are not yet an obligation for income tax reporting purposes.

depreciation An expense that allocates the cost of assets over the period during which they are expected to generate revenues.

disclosure Explanation of all accounting treatments and business issues necessary for a qualified reader of financial statements to understand them.

earned revenue Revenue that has met all of the requirements for recognition in the financial statements whether or not it has been received in cash.

effective income tax rate The rate based on taxes the company is obligated to pay after any adjustments to the statutory tax rate.

expenses Charges against revenues for products purchased or services received other than those that are a cost of the company's own product sold or carried in inventory.

FIFO Method of inventory valuation that assumes that the cost of inventory sold during the period is the cost of the earliest inventory purchased and available for sale in the period.

financial statements The balance sheet, income statement, statement of cash flows, and possibly statement of changes in owners' equity, which together constitute a fair presentation of the company's financial condition at the end of the accounting period and results of operations for the accounting period.

finished goods That part of inventory that consists of completed products ready for sale.

footnotes (to financial statements) The section at end of financial statements where all additional information necessary for a fair presentation is disclosed.

funding The providing of money for purchases of assets, payments of liabilities or reductions in owners' equity.

GAAP Generally Accepted Accounting Principles: The rules which must be followed in the preparation of financial statements for use outside the company.

GAAS Generally Accepted Auditing Standards: The rules which must be followed by independent outside accountants when auditing the financial procedures and statements of a company.

general and administrative expenses Periodic expenses of running the business as opposed to those which can be directly allocated to the cost of a product or a service provided.

going concern Accounting principle which assumes for financial valuation and reporting purposes that a business will continue to operate.

goodwill The excess of the cost of acquiring assets over the book value of the assets acquired. Appears where a business is assumed to have value in excess of the asset values shown on its books.

gross margin Percentage of gross profit to sales.

gross profit Sales less cost of goods sold, representing the profits on product sales which are available to cover selling and general and administrative expenses and to provide a net profit.

historical cost The original cost of an asset unadjusted for subsequent price changes.

Income Statement Financial report showing net income and how it is derived from revenues less all costs and expenses.

incurred expense An expense that represents an obligation for payment even though payment has not yet been made.

individual film forecast Accounting method by which motion picture firms amortize film costs by estimating the amount and timing of receipt of revenues for each film.

insider A person who by virtue of his or her position in a company or relationship to a company is in possession of important company information not available to the public.

intangible assets Assets like patents and franchises that cannot be seen or felt but nevertheless generate revenues.

inventory Product that is either completed or in some stage of production and is to be sold in the ordinary course of a company's business.

inventory supply The number of days the inventory as of a given date would last at the rate of sales for the accounting period ending on that date.

invoice Documentation of a sale and the terms of payment.

LBO (leveraged buy out) A purchase of a company financed by heavy borrowing against the assets of the company being purchased.

leverage The amount of a company's debt in relation to its owners' equity.

liabilities The obligations for which a company has to pay money to others as shown on its balance sheet.

LIFO Method of inventory valuation that assumes that sales during the period consisted of the last inventory purchased or available for sale in the period.

liquidation Sale of all of a company's assets upon termination of its business operations.

liquid ratio *See* quick ratio.

long-term debt Debt that is not due for repayment for more than one year.

marketable securities Securities that have well-defined dollar values and that easily can be converted to cash within one year.

matching Accounting principle that dictates that expenses be charged to the same accounting period as the revenues they generate.

net income Profits of the company after all costs and expenses of the period are subtracted from revenues.

noncurrent assets Assets that are expected to generate revenues over a period exceeding one year.

obsolescence The state of economic uselessness caused by the development of other products that can perform a task far more efficiently.

operating expense An expense of the accounting period related to conducting the ongoing business as opposed to the production of a specific product or service.

operations The company's regular business activities as opposed to investments, financing, or nonrecurring events.

opinion letter Letter in which accountants express their opinion as to whether the financial statements constitute a fair presentation and, if not, what limitations they might have.

overhead Costs and expenses that in the short term are incurred regardless of any fluctuations in the volume of business—that is, they are "fixed" within a reasonable range of fluctuation in volume.

owners' equity The amount of assets left over after all liabilities are deducted, and thus that share of the assets that is left for the owners.

policy acquisition costs The costs an insurance company incurs in order to sell its policies.

prepaid expenses A current asset that represents payment for a service or product at the beginning of an accounting period where the benefit will be received throughout all or a remaining part of the accounting period.

property, plant, and equipment Noncurrent tangible assets of a company that will generate revenues for more than one year.

provision for income taxes Income tax expense for an accounting period derived by applying the effective income tax rate to pretax income.

qualified opinion An opinion of financial statements by independent outside accountants in which there is some reservation about whether the statements constitute a fair presentation.

quick ratio The ratio of cash, cash equivalents, marketable securities, and accounts receivable to current liabilities.

ratios Relationships between various financial data that are useful in analyzing the operations and financial health of the company.

raw materials Materials that have been purchased for inventory but have not yet entered into the production process.

realization The occurrence of an economic transaction that permits the recognition of revenue or income.

recognition Satisfaction of the conditions required for a transaction to meet the accounting requirements necessary to be reported as revenue.

replacement value The value of an asset at the cost of replacing it at current prices.

retained earnings That portion of the accumulated net income of a company that has not been paid out or otherwise reallocated.

return on assets Net income divided by total assets, expressed as a percentage. A measure of the profitability of a company's assets.

return on equity Net income divided by owners' equity, expressed as a percentage. A measure of the profitability of the owners' investment.

revenue Money received or due for products sold or services provided.

reviewed financial statements Financial statements for which the outside independent accountants provide a moderate level of assurance, having checked some accounting procedures but having ·relied heavily on the representations of management.

sales Revenues derived from the exchange of products for cash or an obligation to pay cash.

service companies Companies that receive the predominance of their revenues from providing services as opposed to selling products.

shareholders' equity Owners' equity in a corporation, where the owners are shareholders.

short term In accounting parlance, generally less than one year.

sources of cash Changes in accounts that, other things being equal, will increase cash.

specific identification Process by which each item of inventory is tracked to determine which is sold in an accounting period and which remains in inventory at the end of the period.

Statement of Cash Flows Financial report that shows how much cash has been generated during the accounting period.

Statement of Changes in Financial Position *See* Balance Sheet.

Statement of Changes in Shareholders' or Owners' Equity Financial report that shows the beginning shareholders' or owners' equity, changes occurring during the accounting period, and the ending shareholders' or owners' equity.

statutory income tax rate The prevailing legal tax rate that would be applied to net income before taxes if there were no adjustments to cause pretax income for financial reporting to differ from pretax income for income tax reporting.

straight-line depreciation Depreciation that allocates the same percentage of an asset's cost to each period.

subsidiaries Companies in which another company has a sufficient ownership interest to exercise influence or control.

unamortized film costs That portion of the cost of producing a motion picture which has yet to be amortized and thus still represents an asset on the balance sheet.

uses of cash Changes to accounts that, other things being equal, will result in decreases in cash.

working capital Current assets less current liabilities, or what would be left of current assets if they were used to pay current liabilities.

work in process That portion of inventory that is in the production process but is not yet a finished product.

Index